Tears in Iraq

Hispanic Mother Defies United States Military

Anabelle Valencia

Translated by: Cecilia Bachelier

Note for Librarians: A cataloguing record for this book is available from Library and Archives Canada at www.collectionscanada.ca/amicus/index-e.html
ISBN 1-4251-0566-1

Printed in Victoria, BC, Canada. Printed on paper with minimum 30% recycled fibre. Trafford's print shop runs on "green energy" from solar, wind and other environmentally-friendly power sources.

Offices in Canada, USA, Ireland and UK

Book sales for North America and international:
Trafford Publishing, 6E–2333 Government St.,
Victoria, BC V8T 4P4 CANADA
phone 250 383 6864 (toll-free 1 888 232 4444)
fax 250 383 6804; email to orders@trafford.com
Book sales in Europe:
Trafford Publishing (UK) Limited, 9 Park End Street, 2nd Floor
Oxford, UK OX1 1HH UNITED KINGDOM
phone 44 (0)1865 722 113 (local rate 0845 230 9601)
facsimile 44 (0)1865 722 868; info.uk@trafford.com
Order online at:
trafford.com/06-2324

10 9 8 7 6 5 4 3 2

"Let the children come to me, for theirs is the kingdom of heaven."

Jesus, the Messiah.

DEDICATION

This book is dedicated to all the mothers of the world who have suffered because their children had to go to war. I also dedicate it to the people who made my trip possible: Medea Benjamin, Fernando Suárez del Solar, and Rolande Baker.

Contents

Preface

CURRENT AGONY IN IRAQ

Years have gone by and the Iraqi conflict goes from bad to worse. This is the summer of 2006. The people of the Middle East are living a painful and cruel reality. Civil war is consuming Iraq. I wonder, "Was the invasion worth it?" I think it has left a bad taste in the mouths of most Americans and most people the world over.

The apparently undeclared civil war is among three ancestral and irreconcilable enemies who live in a country carved out by Britain after World War I. They are separated by over 1,300 years of enmity starting in the year 680 with the succession of the Caliphate.

The vast majority of Muslims are **Sunnis**. For them, a Caliph or successor of the Prophet Muhammad can be any devout Muslim who is accepted by the people.

The **Shiites** Muslims, on the other hand, believe a Caliph can only be a direct descendant of the Prophet by his daughter, Fatima, and her husband Ali.

The Sunni live in the central part of Iraq and the Shiites in the south. The **Kurds**, an essentially non-Arabic people, live in the north. For centuries, the Kurds have been hoping to become independent form Iraq. They enjoy autonomy but not sovereignty.

The killings currently taking place in Iraq are the result of sectarian struggles for power within a free and sovereign democracy.

I will not even attempt to predict something I am not sure of. My observations are only the humble thoughts of a mother who has suffered, and continues to suffer, the ravages this war has inflicted upon the Iraqi people.

A few months ago Ator Samo, a dear friend from Baghdad, wrote to me. She implored me to broadcast her plea: "Tell everyone through human rights' organizations all over the world about the inhuman slaughter of my people taking place in Iraq today."

I think during these crucial times President Bush should rethink his idea that he can stop terrorism by simply sending an additional 30,000 American soldiers to Baghdad. Controlling the sectarian violence will not be an easy task. Sooner or later, the foreign forces will tire of the situation and the next U.S. president will have to make the tough decision to withdraw military forces, allowing the Kurds, the Sunnis, and the Shiites to divide their country and create their own independent nations.

PROLOGUE

Anabelle is a woman of temperament. She is passionate in everything she does. All of us who know her can say that she fights for what she wants until she gets it. It is because of her courage that she was able to carry out the deed she has just accomplished. She traveled halfway around the world to see her daughter and challenged the U.S. Army, as well.

I met Anabelle Salcido in Mexico City through my friend, Jesus Venancio Valencia. She was his girlfriend at the time. Both are originally from Sonora, although Anabelle was born in Los Angeles, California. Once married, their two younger children, the main characters in this book, were born in Mexico City. After some setbacks they were able to start their first home. Then, the harsh economic crisis at the beginning of the '80s forced them to leave in search of new horizons. They found themselves immigrating to the United States.

Anabelle's children, Jessika, Giselle, and Chuveny, grew up first in Riverside, California and then in

Tucson, Arizona. It was about five years ago when the younger children, in search of opportunities, scholarships, and a higher education, joined the United States Army. When the Twin Towers were attacked both children were sent to Iraq. Chuveny was deployed to Baghdad as a paratrooper with the 82nd Airborne Division. Giselle, a transportation specialist with the 4th Infantry Division, was in charge of transporting prisoners of war from the Sunni region of Tikrit, Saddam Hussein's hometown, to the infamous Abu Ghraib prison.

If war is perilous and of much concern to everyone, it is so much more so to the parents of two soldiers.

The official end of the war did not bring any peace of mind to Anabelle and Jesus. At that time they were informed that their children's stay in the war zone was not going to be for six months, as originally promised, but was going to be for an indefinite length of time.

Anabelle started to protest against the war, the United States government, and its lies. She joined peace groups that demanded the return home of American soldiers. Her struggle was echoed in the pacifist organization, Global Exchange.

Hosted by Global Exchange, Anabelle was one of a group of nine civilians who would travel to Iraq on a peace mission not authorized by the U.S. government. Her position was to take the Iraqi people a message of solidarity and peace; to tell them there were those who did not agree with the war and who asked for the return of our soldiers.

Early in December, 2003 the group traveled to Jordan. From there they were transported to Baghdad. Anabelle did not have permission or an invitation to visit her daughter. However, the day after she arrived she let them know she would show up at the military base. The group traveled to the city of Tikrit accompanied by a group of reporters from both Western and Arab countries.

Anabelle arrived at the military base on December 5, asking to see her soldier daughter. She was not received cordially. An officer accompanied by a police dog informed her that her daughter was out on a mission in Baghdad. "This is the Army and she is in good health," Anabelle was informed in an attempt to dissuade her.

The scene was not a pleasant one. Anabelle informed them that she would not move from there until she saw her daughter. Trying to resolve the situation, they called an American-trained Iraqi policeman. "We have orders to arrest any protestors," he said. A crying Anabelle showed them pictures of her daughter. "It is terrible that the Americans do not let you see your beloved daughter," he said.

With true Iraqi friendliness, the police chief confided, "If this is how they treat their own people, imagine how they treat us." Taking advantage of the presence of the foreign press, some policemen criticized the invasion saying, "Americans promised a lot: democracy, liberty, security ... now we have none of that. We were better off before. We all preferred Saddam's times." That is just what the Iraqi guardians of the peace said.

After several hours of protest with the support and sympathy of the Iraqis, the Army officer approached her and promised to get her permission to visit the next day.

With great emotion and fear, Anabelle returned the next day disguised as an Iraqi woman. After almost three years of not seeing her daughter, Anabelle was allowed to visit with her for only two hours. It was a glorious time. Anabelle's voice still quivers at the memory of all that she saw in Iraq and everything she went through to see her daughter.

Since then Anabelle has given press conferences in New York, Washington, and Tucson. She will not remove the button she wears that says, "Bring the soldiers home NOW." Not until her children are back.

Dr. Nicolas Pineda Pablos
Investigator and Political Analyst

1

A MOTHER'S HEART

It was a day like any other when my 20-year-old daughter told me, "Mom, I'm going to enlist in the Army." My reaction was, "Don't do it. You could be sent to war." She answered, "No, Mom, I don't think there will be a war."

I did not want my daughter to enlist in the Army. But, what a surprise it was when a few days later my 19-year-old son, Chuveny, came in and gave me the same news. His sister had convinced him to join the armed forces, too. Can you imagine what a shock that was for me?

I could not dissuade them from their plans; they were of legal age and I could do nothing to impede it. My husband supported their decision and then, finally, I did the same.

Both my children left for basic training at about the same time. Giselle was sent to South Carolina and Chuveny to Fort Benning, Georgia. Every day, on my way to work I prayed for them. I prayed to God that nothing would happen to them and that they would be able to complete their basic training successfully. And so it was. They graduated at different times and we were not able to attend either of their ceremonies. We were raising our eight-month-old grandson and it was impossible for us to be there with them.

All this happened in the summer of 2000. Afterwards, Giselle was sent to Germany for two years and during that time she could not get leave to come home. Chuveny went on to North Carolina.

All was going well. My children said that when they were discharged, the Army would make good on their promises of benefits and money for a college education. That was the main reason they joined the Army.

2

TERRORISM IN THE UNITED STATES

The infamous September 11, 2001 came. The day Al-Qaeda terrorism hit the financial heart of the United States. As I watched the two planes crashing into the Twin Towers of the World Trade Center in New York I immediately thought of my children.

I started to cry and said to my husband, "My children are going to war. My children are going to war." My mother's heart sensed it.

I knew it from the very start. The government of George W. Bush would not permit this and do nothing. We were being attacked and we had to defend ourselves. I never thought this war or conflict would be against a tyrant and, even less so, that the war would be over control of Iraq's huge oil supplies.

When it was announced that Osama Bin Laden was the one behind the attacks on the Twin Towers, I thought the U.S. would go after him and bring him to justice, but I was wrong. At that time I did not know about the enormous economic interests that bound the Bush family, the Bin Laden family, and the royal house of Saudi Arabia – those despots covered in oil who have had the United States government eating out of their hands since the first oil embargo in 1973.

Inspectors were sent to Iraq. Days went by and they found nothing. Since they could not find anything I thought there would be no war and that they would keep Saddam quiet by other means.

Not much later our children called from their bases and tried to calm us down. Giselle requested a transfer to Texas. She was tired of the cold in Germany. Her transfer was granted but first she had to reenlist for another two years. In February she was transferred to the 4th Infantry Division at Fort Hood, Texas.

Every time my children called I cried bitterly. I knew they would go to war very soon. And so it was. On March 12, 2003 my son called to say goodbye. His parachute unit of the 82nd Airborne received orders to deploy to Iraq. He said, "Mother, everything will be alright. Please don't cry. We're going after Saddam Hussein and his weapons of mass destruction."

A few days later our daughter Giselle called to say that she, too, was going to Iraq but with the 4th Infantry Division. She said, "Mom, remember, if anything happens to me, it's because I'm fighting for a noble cause." I gave her my blessing as I had done with my son and asked her a thousand times to be careful and told her we would be waiting for them.

When all this happened we had already started marching in the streets of Tucson, Arizona in several protests against the war. But as we realized that the war was imminent, we supported soldiers, in general, and our children, in particular, but not the war. We thought that the egotistical Saddam could have fallen in many different ways. However, for the Pentagon "hawks" this was a long-awaited opportunity to control the black gold and there was only one option: military intervention.

Intelligence agencies wanted to obtain something that did not exist. They knew very well it was a pretense and that there were no weapons of mass destruction. The government, always trying to pull the wool over our eyes, went ahead with the invasion and the destruction. Under the pretense of destroying something that did not exist, we too became criminals and terrorists. We became the world's policemen. Damn wars that only bring misery, destruction, and death!

We knew that our son was stationed near Baghdad, but we had not heard from our daughter. We did not hear from her for several months.

3

THE TAKING OF BAGHDAD

One night, as always, while I watching the news to see what was happening in the war, Saddam Hussein sent a message to all American mothers. His words were: "All American mothers will cry tears of blood." I felt chills and fear that I had never felt before. After a few minutes, I prayed, placing my children and everyone in Iraq in God's hands. I imagined it would happen as it had in the '80s when Iraq launched a bloody war against its neighbor, Iran, over the control of Shat-el-Arab, a strategic stretch of land with access to the Gulf and over the control of oil exportation through that area. During that time Shiite communities in the south of Iraq were reprimanded by the Hussein regime; but the Kurd communities were reprimanded much more. The Kurds, an essentially non-Arabic community, took advantage of the situation to rebel against Saddam's regime. They were so harshly reprimanded that

Hussein authorized the use of chemical warfare in several communities indiscriminately murdering men, women, and children. Five thousand died in one community.

This was why I thought as we entered Baghdad there would be terrible slaughter. Just knowing the American soldiers had taken the city's international airport filled me with anxiety and desperation. At one point I thought, "Go ahead. Get it over with."

I knew my son was in a nearby city, but we did not know exactly where. We were only guided by news reports. The rest was pure conjecture on our part.

4

PHONE CALL FROM KUWAIT

The war continued and we had not heard from Chuveny, but we did know that Giselle was in Kuwait. A few days later we heard on the news that the 82nd Airborne Division was south of Baghdad. In my desperation I imagined my son dropping from the sky in a parachute. I knew he was in a lot of danger since he was in Special Forces. My biggest prayer was, "Jesus, in You I trust." I repeated it over and over.

One night Giselle called from Kuwait to tell us that the 4th Infantry Division to which she was attached would leave in a few hours for Baghdad. Just a few days earlier many American soldiers had been ambushed and murdered. We also had heard about the kidnapping of Jessica Lynch. We saw on the television the horrors of war and the suffering of millions of American families. We saw it live, thanks to the magic of satellite television.

How was this mistake possible? A military caravan

made its way towards Baghdad. It was a very dark night and a huge sandstorm impeded all visibility. Then, the vehicle took a wrong turn and ran right into an ambush. Tremendous gunfire started, taking the lives of more of our heroes, among them Laurie Piestewa, the first female soldier to die in combat, a Native American mother of two from Arizona. Jessica Lynch was luckier. Wounded and battered, Pfc. Lynch was abandoned in a hospital room in Nasiriyah until an Iraqi doctor felt compassion for her situation and informed a military commander. From that moment on her rescue was planned and, as we all know, it was an exciting success.

My daughter once told me, "If something happens to me and my company and I live through it and I'm in the hands of Iraqi rebels, I'd beg to be killed. I wouldn't want to be tortured and raped."

That night I could not sleep. I got up and prayed. I remember, on one occasion, going into the living room where we keep a picture of my mother-in-law, Mama Machú, God rest her soul. I touched the image of her face and begged her to intercede for me before God for her grandchildren. May He watch over them and everyone else in combat." Later I awoke my husband and said, "Honey, my children. My children!" I remember him turning to me and saying, "Not a single leaf moves from a tree without the will of God. Come to bed. Our children are safe." At that moment I cried and asked forgiveness from the Lord for not having enough faith.

5

MANIFESTATION OF GOD

It was the second week of the war. Everyday I had a free hour at work, so I would go to my car and listen to the news. For ten minutes I would sit and listen about how the war was going and then pray to God with great devotion.

During these moments I would find myself concentrating deeply on my pledges. I would pray to Christ for my loved ones and for everyone who found themselves in this horrible conflict against the Iraqi people. I would think about the thousands upon thousands of families who were in the same situation that I was and pray for us all equally. I prayed for those who had already given their lives to defend this country and for their families, asking the Lord to comfort them in their sorrow.

As the minutes passed my prayers became more pleasant. Once, I was feeling them with so much fervor that I suddenly felt the hand of God pass over my shoulder and touch my heart. I felt a marvelous peace. Without saying a word He said, "Everything is alright. Everything is alright." For a few seconds I felt a marvelous peace and I cried and thanked God from the bottom of my heart for His visitation. The Lord filled me with happiness and I told Him, "Whatever You decide, my Lord, I will accept with resignation, whatever it is. My children are yours."

For the first time I accepted that my children did not belong to me, that they were on loan to me and only God could decide what He would do with their lives. I promised I would accept whatever happened to my children in Iraq. I would never again doubt that my children were in His hands. Just a few days later I again had the privilege and the grace of my Lord's manifestation.

That day I was again praying when, like a hand passing over my heart, I felt God's presence telling me, "Do not worry. All is well." By this I understood that my children were protected from all danger and that they would return safe and sound.

Mamá Machú

6

INVITATION TO IRAQ

One exceptional day in Tucson I was talking with my workmate, Rolande Baker, a special education teacher at Sunnyside High School in Tucson, Arizona. Rolande Baker is a great woman in all senses of the word. She fights for truth and justice. She is intelligent, courageous, and has a great sense of humor. She is extremely honest; nothing halfway with her. She gives her all and asks nothing in return. To me she was an angel sent from heaven during some of the most difficult times of my life. My pain was her pain, my suffering hers. Ms. Baker is a veteran peace activist; so, of course, she is against this irrational war. She fights day after day for our soldiers' return and for an end to this conflict.

That day in Tucson she told me about a man named Fernando Suárez del Solar, the father of one of the first Hispanic soldiers killed in Iraq. He was coming to Tucson. Ms. Baker, as she is affectionately known, asked me if I would like to host Mr. Suárez along with a few other families whose children are currently in Iraq. I loved the idea and immediately accepted.

The day arrived and the meeting was both exciting and productive. Mr. Suárez told us about the circumstances of his only son's death and we spoke about how illegal and unnecessary this war is.

He mentioned that in a few weeks he would be traveling to the Middle East with a group of people who were taking a message of peace to the Iraqi people. Once there, he was going to look for the place where his beloved son had given his life.

He said he could take two people from Arizona and told us that if anyone was interested we should let him know. The next day Mr. Suárez spoke at Sunnyside High School with both students and teachers. I really admired him. I felt his charisma firsthand and his great pain at having lost his only son.

Fernando was the second angel who came into my life. A few days after his visit I called to say that I wanted to accompany the group. Thanks to him I was able to go to Iraq in search of my children.

A few days before calling Fernando, I mentioned to my husband that I wanted to go to Iraq. My husband was in complete agreement. I went and knelt down before my Christ and prayed, "Lord Jesus, You know I want to go and look for my two loved ones in Iraq, but You also know I have nothing: no passport, no money, no leave of absence from work. I would be traveling at a time of great danger and would be risking my life. My Lord, if You think I should go, please arrange it so that I can."

In a matter of days everything fell into place. I would leave for the conflict zone on November 29, 2003.

7

NOVEMBER 3, 2003

On November 2, 2003 an American helicopter transporting troops from Fallujah to Baghdad was shot down. Sixteen soldiers were killed and twenty injured. I could not believe it. Perhaps our son was among them. I thought of the thousands of families who are in the same boat as I am. I knew Giselle was in Tikrit, but Chuveny was frequently moved around.

I felt powerless, yet enraged at this disgraceful action. I was afraid, too, and considered not going on the trip. I thought, "If I don't go and something happens to my children, I would never forgive myself." I chose not to be a coward. Just the opposite, I would search for my children and take a message of peace to the Iraqi people. Opportunity knocks but once and one has to take advantage of it.

Two days later Giselle called and asked me not to come to Iraq. Things were getting uglier and more dangerous with each passing day and she did not want me to risk my life. However, I would not change my mind. The trip was already set up. We would leave for Iraq on November 29, 2003.

My son called, too. He was very upset. He said he didn't want me to come, that the trip was crazy. He begged me, "Mother, if you end up coming, don't look for me. It would be embarrassing if my company knew my mother was coming to look for me!" Just to calm him down I promised not to come looking for him. However, my intentions were to leave no stone unturned. I would go to the ends of the earth to be with my children. Chuveny came home to Tucson on two weeks' leave. On our way back to the airport he reminded me, "Mother, you're not going on your trip, are you?" I replied, "Son, everything's ready for my trip to Iraq. I go in search of your sister." He said, "That's why I'm here. I came to convince you not to go." I responded, "Nothing will change my mind. God bless you, son."

My son was sent to Iraq three times during the war.

The day came when I had to leave for Iraq. I would be traveling to the Middle East, to Saddam Hussein's own country. I was happy but somewhat nervous. I was traveling into the unknown and did not know whether I would come back alive or in a body bag. A few days earlier I had asked Ms. Baker, "Do you think I'll come back?" She assured me, "Of course you will. They told me if anything happens to you, I'll be held responsible." My answer was, "This is my decision and I go at my own risk."

The American government had already warned us that they would not be held accountable for anything that happened to us. However, several congressmen had given Fernando letters for high-ranking military officials in Iraq, ordering them to receive us.

Much to my surprise, on November 29, 2003, the *Arizona Daily Star* published an article about my trip that made front-page headlines.

On the plane to Minneapolis, Minnesota everything came off without a hitch. There, we changed planes and were bound for Amsterdam where we had agreed to meet. At 10 o'clock the following morning, after traveling 5,400 miles, I finally got there! I loved the Amsterdam airport, how beautiful with its own hotel inside. Paris doesn't even have an airport as beautiful as Amsterdam's. The first person I saw was Fernando, my dear friend and traveling companion. I felt very fortunate to have met him. Thanks to him and to many other people, my trip in search of my children was becoming a reality. Fernando was the first person I saw when I came into the waiting room. He was already waiting for me with his kind smile and his great charisma.

We went to meet Medea Benjamin, my third angel, an intelligent and brave woman who is very active in causes in favor of world peace. She is a veteran activist and founder of Global Exchange, an independent organization that fights for human rights all over the world. She is also cofounder of

Code Pink. She was accompanied by Sean Penn, the famous and handsome actor, who was traveling to Baghdad as an independent reporter and would be staying at the Palestine Hotel.

The four of us were sitting at a table. Sean Penn asked me if I wanted something to drink and he kindly brought me a soda. He invited us to his room. I gladly accepted and took a shower. It was like a refreshing dream. I felt lucky because the harsh emotions of our journey hadn't really begun, yet.

It was eight o'clock at night on the November 30, 2003 in the Amsterdam airport when I heard the news that Spain had just been attacked. My fear then was that we would not make it to Baghdad alive.

8

AT THE JORDANIAN-IRAQI BORDER

After nine hours of traveling from Amman, Jordan through the desert we finally arrived at the Iraqi border. We immediately realized there were no American soldiers guarding the border.

I thought somehow when I saw military personnel, I would be in touch with my children, but I was wrong. What I did notice was that our luggage was never checked. We could have crossed over with weapons or explosives and we would have gone unnoticed.

What kind of orders did American officers have to give to make sure the border was safe? Catching the terrorists coming into Iraq? How illusive a goal!

Forty miles from Baghdad and very close to Falluja, we were detained at an American military checkpoint which had combat cars and a tank blocking the road. There were dozens of Iraqi cars waiting, as well. Some of us got out of our cars to take pictures.

This brought out a group of skeptical American soldiers, pointing their M16 rifles and shouting at us, "Stop! Identify yourselves! Who the hell are you?"

Immediately, Medea told them, "We are Americans and we are here on a peace mission for the Iraqi people. We are fighting to get you guys home soon."

Meanwhile, the waiting Iraqis beginning to get restless, making the soldiers even more nervous. One of them told us that the horrible Samara ambushes had happened just the day before and things were tense. Two American military patrols had been ambushed simultaneously there. Fedayeen wearing black uniforms had carried out the attacks urban-guerrilla style.

Moments later another tank rode up and a sensible lieutenant made the decision to let the Iraqis go through. He took us to the side of the road to interrogate us. That is when we heard about the Samara ambushes the day before and why they thought the Red Cross vehicle in front might have hidden explosives.

I was able to see the soldiers in their tanks with their boyish faces, maybe eighteen or nineteen years old, tense and nervous. You could see tiredness in their faces. I thought of my children and felt full of pride. My two loved ones were in the same situation as these boys, risking their lives to give the Iraqi people a better life.

A short time later, Fernando talked to a young Mexican man who lived in Chicago named Luis Gutierrez. He advised us to be very cautious and not to feel too confident in Baghdad. He gave Fernando his mother's phone number so that Fernando could call her when we returned to Washington. Fernando did just that. However, when he called her, at first she thought something had happened to her son, but Fernando calmed her down and told her that her son was well and he sent her a big hug and a kiss.

We said goodbye to the soldiers and we could hear a confrontation in the distance taking place between Iraqi rebels and American soldiers.

There were times when the drivers drove 100 mph as we passed through very dangerous places where we could be attacked. All of a sudden, they started racing each another. A piece of luggage fell off the car in front of us. The driver swerved to avoid it, almost rolling the car.

There were moments when I thought we would not make it to Baghdad alive. On the other hand, we were happy and enjoying the beautiful Iraqi desert.

9

ARRIVAL IN BAGHDAD

We drove for twelve hours by road from Amman to Baghdad through an unending desert. We saw long lines of trucks transporting oil out of the country, heavily guarded by the American military. Going the other way, we saw the trucks returning empty, equally guarded by the military.

We finally arrived in the beautiful and heroic city of Baghdad. It was about five o'clock in the afternoon December 1, 2003. The radiant sun was still shining on the city, on its wide and clean streets, and on the two-storied homes with high walls around them. We were told these homes had belonged to the dictator's family members.

The scenery started to change little by little as we made our way downtown. There, we found lots of trash on the streets, bombed-out buildings and people driving crazily – many going the wrong way on one-way streets. There was no authority on the streets and everyone did what they wanted. We immediately noticed that the American convoys and tanks had preference over everyone. This bothered the Iraqis tremendously.

Days went by and we became aware of the fact that a majority of the people feel deep anger and hatred towards the military occupation. They told us so openly. At the same time they thanked the United States for freeing them from the yoke of Saddam Hussein.

10

ASSASSINATION OF AN IRAQI LEADER

We finally arrived at the Agadir Hotel, where we were staying, just a few blocks from the Palestine. We found a group of German and French newsmen already waiting for us with television cameras. From that moment on it became clear that we were being taken seriously. The press was with us the whole trip.

When the news journalists finished with their interviews we left for our first encounter. We were told that we would be visiting an Iraqi family. We drove in two very old cars so as not to attract attention. The press followed closely in different cars. We turned onto an unpaved street and parked farther up from the house. Across the street was the local mosque of that poor neighborhood. Outside the house was a white banner in commemoration of the death of Mohammed Ghazi Al-Kabi, leader of the Al-Sadr city council, who had been killed by an American soldier. This is where the many important events of the week took place.

We were greeted at the door by several people dressed in tunics and wearing turbans. We were guided to a small room with no furniture where removed our shoes. Later, we were escorted to a larger room, again with no furniture, only cushions. The ground was covered with huge carpets of many colors. We immediately started taking out the messages written by American children. The messages, among others, included: "Peace," "Love to our brothers," "The United Sates loves you," "No more blood," "No more deaths of innocent children," and "Stop the war."

As soon as both the press and our group were settled, the father, Ghazi Al-Kabi, introduced himself and started talking to us through an interpreter. He told us that an American soldier had assassinated his 26-year-old son. The reason for the crime was that the boy had shown up at his office unannounced. The American soldier did not like seeing him there so he shot him point-blank, killing him instantly.

At the end of the conversation Medea Benjamin and Fernando Suárez del Solar offered the family our public condolences and begged forgiveness on behalf of the American people for the tragedy. In response the father introduced us to his other son, a tall, light-skinned, nice-looking young man who looked a lot like his brother, whose photograph we happened to notice. They thanked us and, as a token of their appreciation, offered us a small cup of tea symbolizing that we were welcome in their home.

Minutes later we were shown into a dimly lit room, again no furniture, with traditional carpets on the floor. In the middle of the room sat a tall and slender woman dressed in black from head to foot. We could only see a part of her beautiful face on which we noticed deep pain, the pain of a mother who has lost her beloved son. These people's pain was deep because they felt offended by the occupying army. In the entire year after, they had received only a minimal apology from the military and no aid.

Reflecting on the role of Iraqi women, I would say Iraqi women occupy a low level in their society. I understood why there were no women at the first meeting. No one pays any attention to them. Women have no voice in making the important decisions of the home.

A day after our visit, the commander of the local military base visited the family and asked, "Why were there so many lights and television cameras here the night before?" Very soon they returned with $10,000 and the promise that the family would receive $3,000 every month as compensation for the death of their son. However, they were not to give any more information to the press. We were very surprised by the large sum of money our visit brought in. And it was only the first day of the trip.

Some of our friends were taken to visit a hospital for the elderly and the rest of us went back to the hotel. It was about ten o'clock in the evening. I was starving. So, I went down to the desk and exchanged American money for Iraqi money. I walked around a little and found a restaurant. Somehow, I managed to order something to eat. They served more than ten dishes of food. I hardly ate any. Just

looking at all that food made me feel full. I paid and went straight to my room to sleep.

11

SCHOOLS AND HOSPITALS

We found ourselves in a country that was a complete disaster. Thousands of people had no jobs and no way to feed their families. Electricity functioned at only 50% capacity. Telephone stations destroyed during the war had not been repaired. The water was not safe to drink. Many hospitals lacked the basic equipment and medications necessary to operate properly. The schools had no lights, no air conditioning, and no books. There were piles of trash in the streets. In a country rolling in oil, the lines for gas were five to seven hours long in Baghdad and in other cities.

During our visit to the Al-Awsiga elementary school we found a deplorable situation: the building was in dire need of repair. It was unsanitary and had no electricity. The teachers had neither books nor the most basic tools to function. The students gathered in a patio area and we gave out toys and letters written by American children. The letters expressed solidarity with them and their suffering. The students chanted, "We want peace. We want peace," for about five minutes.

It was nearly five o'clock in the afternoon on December 3, 2003 when we arrived at the Iskan hospital. They specialize in children with leukemia. These poor children still suffer the effects of the Persian Gulf War of 1991 and remain in a state of total abandonment by both their own government and the U.S. government.

At the hospital we were greeted by both local and foreign press. Many people were there. The hospital was in bad condition. Suddenly, an Iraqi woman surprised me. She was dressed in black from head to foot and was carrying a child only a few months old. The baby was wrapped in a small blanket and the mother was desperately trying to tell me something I could not understand. I asked the interpreter to tell me what she was saying. She translated, "The woman says her son is very sick, to please take him and have him cured. Save him from death." I was shocked and the only thing I could think of saying was, "I would like to help you but I cannot take your son." I felt sorry as I handed him back to her. I certainly was not in a condition to bring the child back to the United States with me.

I remember the press interviewing us as we walked through the rooms. We got to where the children were, but we did not know what their illnesses were. Fernando had brought a large suitcase with lots of clothes donated in California for the children of Iraq. Before long I found myself handing out clothes to the sick children. I was taken to see a child who seemed about seven. He was very thin and his eyes were sunken because of his illness. His mother was seated at his bedside. Medea said, "Look at the condition of this child." She uncovered him and I saw a big ulcerated area on his left thigh. It was over three inches in diameter. I could not believe what I saw. The boy tried to cover himself so we would not see his private parts. I could not take it. I found a place were I could be alone and cried. Fernando was profoundly moved also. Medea observed, "Oh, you Mexicans are such crybabies!"

I was still shaking from what I had seen: a child with leukemia in such a terrible condition. These are the consequences left behind by damn wars for which, in the end, only the innocent have to pay the price. These poor souls are what is left from the Persian Gulf War of 1991. The United States government does not help them because they are not part of this war.

Going through most of the hospital we proved to ourselves that it was in very bad condition, indeed. They had no medications and no medical equipment. The doctors and other personnel had been working with no pay for the past six months. We took on the task of promising that their demands would be taken to Washington.

I remember one child in particular. He was about eleven and his name was Hussein. He asked me for candy or a gift but I had nothing to give him right then. He took my hand, hugged me, and in his language told me he loved me like his mother. I hugged him back. The hospital worker kept sending him away and he kept coming back to hug me again. Even from the car, I saw him waving goodbye and throwing kisses to me. I did the same until I lost sight of him.

During the trip I thought, "There's nothing more beautiful than a child's smile. Someday I'll return with many gifts and candy for all the children. I'll come back when it's different; without violence and with a democracy where one can come and go freely without fear of bombings." I thought a lot about these things.

It was at about seven in the evening that same day when we arrived at the Al-Jazeera television studios in Baghdad. In the lobby we met a desperate Iraqi father. One day, his eleven-year-old son was playing soccer on the sidewalk in front of his home. He saw some Coalition military cars coming and, as a joke and without thinking, he threw the ball at one of the cars causing chaos inside the car. One soldier's instinctive reaction was to shoot at the boy. He wounded him in the leg. When the soldier realized what had happened, he started yelling and screaming, blaming himself for his mistake.

The desperate father was at the studio asking

for donations to pay for his son's medical bills. We collected some money for him. He thanked us by placing his hand over his heart.

Al-Awsiga Elementary School in Baghdad.

Chuveny at Fort Bragg, days before going to Iraq.

Chuveny posing with captured enemy weapons found in the Al-Dora district, Baghdad, June 2003.

Group photo in front of our hotel in Baghdad, shortly before departure to Jordan.

My daughter Giselle shortly before leaveing Fort Hood, Texas en route to Kuwait

Seizing the opportunity for a photo during a break from training exercises in Kuwait, prior to the invasion.

Fernado Suarez Del Solar manifesting against the war in Iraq. The crosses represent more than two thousand American Soldiers who have perished, amongst them, his son Jesus Suarez del Solar Navarro

12

PAUL BREMER

Chief of the Coalition's Provisional Authority

Day 3. It was 11:30 in the morning when we entered Baghdad's super-guarded Green Zone, seat of the Provisional Authority whose chief was Mr. Paul Bremer. To get there we had to go through four military checkpoints. Each required us to show documents and IDs. Even our cameras had to be checked. The Provisional Authority was located in one of the most luxurious palaces of the former dictator. Huge marble columns dominated the entrance. Inside there were beautiful chandeliers and luxurious curtains.

Within minutes we had an interview with Abdul Aziz Al-Hakim, leader of the Supreme Council for the Islamic Revolution in Iraq. He told us of the great appreciation his organization feels towards the United States. But he also expressed the sentiment of the Iraqi people by saying, "Thank you for liberating us from the tyrant Saddam Hussein, but we do not want a city permanently occupied by the American troops."

He was nice enough to answer all our questions and shared his opinion that the Iraqi people, in spite of the shortages and the pain and destruction, desire to build their own democracy. He said, "It is not the job of the Americans to do this. It is up to us."

Then Paul Bremer came in. We wanted to talk to Mr. Bremer because we hoped to get his authorization to interview General Ricardo Sanchez, commander of the ground forces in Iraq.

Mr. Bremer promised to get us the interview, but it was never to take place. General Sanchez proved too elusive. Mr. Bremer invited us to a sumptuous buffet with trays full of fruit, plates of lamb and chicken, and an assortment of desserts. No doubt it was the best food in Baghdad.

As we left, while walking towards our vehicles, we saw a huge convoy of American tanks coming up the street. We could tell they in command of the streets because as they passed the children were afraid. I was filled with emotion: very proud and, at the same time, wanting my loved ones to return home soon.

At one point I was so happy I said, "They are wonderful, beautiful." Someone from the group responded, "How can you say that? Don't you see they're here to kill?" I immediately responded with tears in my eyes, "It's just that I'm looking for my son." It was going to be impossible to find my son. They all looked so alike in their uniforms and helmets. I would never find him this way.

Since we were unable to get permission from the commander, we headed out on our own.

Our friend, Mike Lopercio of Phoenix, Arizona accompanied by Vietnam veteran John Grant left for a dangerous military base near Falluja hoping to hug his son, Tony.

I headed off to Tikrit, Saddam Hussein's hometown, to see my daughter Giselle.

Bod Woodruff, reporter for ABC (center), accompanied by Fernando del Solar and an Iraqi official (left) just before an audience with the Provisional Chief of Authority in Iraq.

Paul Bremer, Provisional Chief of Authority of the Coalition in Iraq

13

TESTIMONY IN DIWANIYA

Thursday, December 4, 2003. Very early in the morning we noticed several Iraqi women dressed in black from head to foot who were staying at the same hotel. We were told they came from different places to pray at the mosques. Friday is a big day for Muslims, much like Sunday is for us. It is a holy day, the only day of the week when no one works. They were wearing so many clothes that I wondered if they could be hiding bombs underneath.

Five times a day, from mosques' loudspeakers, we would hear voices calling everyone to prayer. One day from the hotel stairway, we watched two people suddenly throw themselves on the floor and pray towards Mecca. We thought it strange and could only stare at each another in amazement.

The day before, I asked Fernando if I could accompany him on his trip to Diwaniya, 110 miles south of Baghdad. He was going to search for the exact spot his son gave his life for his country. Fernando's son, Jesus, died barely eight months before on March 27, 2003. I believed I could in some way alleviate his suffering if something occurred that might be very painful for him. I could help ease his pain by giving him words of encouragement at the right time.

Bob Woodruff, a reporter for ABC, was embedded with Delta Company of the Marines' First Division the day Fernando's son Jesús stepped on a grenade and was fatally wounded. A few days earlier, Woodruff had interviewed Jesus, not knowing that the next time he would see him he would be wounded and waiting for help to arrive. Help came too late. Jesús Suarez del Solar Navarro died in a helicopter on the way to the hospital.

Fernando, Bob Woodruff, Bob's cameraman, and I left for Diwaniya in a armored vehicle. We noticed that the rear window had bullet holes in it, probably made by Iraqi rebels. After traveling for over two hours we reached our destination and found ourselves surrounded by camels. It was a deserted area just north of what was once an ammunition depot of Saddam Hussein's Republican Guard.

"The United States artillery shot mortars and grenades into that area believing it housed fedayeen," Bob explained.

We started walking across the desert, but it was muddy. Someone took my arm. He could see that because of the mud I was having trouble getting to the place where Jesús was killed. Our friend, Fernando, asked for five minutes alone to pray in memory of his son. He placed a crucifix on the spot. The crucifix was later returned to a church in Baghdad. Fernando asked me to help him gather some soil to put in plastic bags. He wanted to take some to Escondido, California where he planned to plant a white rosebush in the park near his home.

We continued walking, picking up food bags left by the soldiers. I remember Fernando finding a small bottle of Tabasco sauce and telling me, "This was Jesús' favorite salsa."

We started crying and I tried to give Fernando some words of comfort. I remember that in my pain and impotence I said, "Damn war! It's killing our children." We walked a few more steps and Fernando fainted. It was then I noticed we were being filmed. The reporter yelled to his crew to stop filming. They turned off the cameras.

Farther up ahead we saw foxholes and were told they were used by American soldiers to hide from Iraqi rebels.

I felt great sorrow for Fernando. His pain could not be greater. The soil we collected is drenched with his beloved son's blood. Jesus gave up his life so Iraqi children could have a better one.

Fernando subsequently started the Proyecto Guerrero Azteca (Aztec Warrior Project) in honor of his son. He travels throughout the U.S. and the world with a clear message for all young people: "Don't enlist in the armed forces. Enroll in a university." He has become the voice of Hispanics against military recruitment.

Rest in peace, Jesus Suarez del Solar Navarro.
(November 16, 1982 - March 27, 2003)

14

CONFRONTATION AT TIKRIT

Friday, December 5, 2003. I got up at six o'clock in the morning, as usual. After returning from Diwaniya the previous evening, we still had quite an itinerary ahead. We worked until ten that night. I was dead tired and went to my room.

My bed had a wooden base with a thin mat on top. It was hard as rock, but I was so tired it felt divine. After saying my prayers I went to bed. I thanked God for this day and asked him to protect my children and all the soldiers that were here. As I lay there I couldn't help but listen to the stillness of my room; but, as usual, I could hear shots and explosions every now and again.

The next day I found out an American soldier had been killed in a store. It hurt me deeply, knowing that people were dying and we could do nothing. I felt impotent, frustrated, and indignant at the deaths of so many innocent people.

When I got up I made the sign of the cross and

started to get ready as best as I could. I thought today would be the day I would find my daughter Giselle.

At seven o'clock, the press was already in the dining room with their reflectors and bright lights. I chose to sit with my back to them. Their constant presence sometimes made it difficult to eat. Halfway through breakfast, a female reporter came up and asked me if she could accompany us to Tikrit. I saw no reason why she couldn't. She happily thanked me. I couldn't figure out why. Our friends Mike Lopercio and John Grant were also leaving for their destination: Fallujah, in search of Mike's son. I understand things went quite well for them.

We traveled in old cars to Tikrit dressed as Iraqi women; our heads covered with black cloths and accompanied by our Iraqi driver, Sam. Medea Benjamin, Gael Murphy (in charge of taping all the events), Sam, and I were the participants in the Tikrit encounter. The press was following close behind. Gael filmed me, asking questions about how I would react when I saw my daughter.

I was enjoying watching the Apache helicopters as they guarded the road. All of a sudden, on the left I saw an American tank burning on the side of the road. There were several soldiers standing around it. I started to cry and remember saying, "I hope nothing happened to them." I thought of my daughter Giselle transporting prisoners of war from Tikrit to Baghdad. I could feel a remnant of the danger of the bomb explosion. The danger I felt for us was the same. If they knew we were Americans, we might be attacked.

Halfway there we were detained at a military checkpoint. We did not know why. Perhaps there was a confrontation with Iraqi rebels up ahead.

The wait seemed endless. After about thirty minutes Sam decided to take another route. I took some more pictures along that road. Coming into Tikrit, Sam drove one block past the military base before realizing it: the base is so far out of the city. We parked the car and I took pictures of Saddam Hussein's castle. The reporters behind us let us know we might be attacked just for filming.

The day before, I sent an e-mail to the military base stating that I was coming to visit my daughter. I never got a reply. It was early afternoon when we arrived at General Headquarters of the 4th Infantry Division (Task Force Iron Horse) – the occupation forces located in the difficult Sunni Triangle.

Our reception at the military base was not at all agreeable. In fact, it was very hostile. An American soldier came out with a huge German shepherd shouting at us to leave, that we should not be here. Other soldiers came out with M16 rifles. "Step back," they ordered.

We took two steps backward but still seemed to be in the same place. Suddenly, we were surrounded by the press. I really did not know where they came from. The soldiers were furious, screaming at a reporter to stop filming and to surrender the tape. She refused and made a show of erasing it. However, she continued filming when their backs were turned. They did not say anything.

We identified ourselves. I told them I was here to see my daughter. A soldier who refused to identify himself said, "Ma'am, your daughter's OK. She's very healthy. She's a soldier and is on a mission to Baghdad." My daughter and I had passed each other on the road! I told him, "I've come halfway around the world to hug my daughter and I will not leave until I've seen her."

After the American soldiers fully understood the situation, they called the American-trained Tikrit police. Capt. Mohammed Ali Hussein of the Regional Police said, "We have orders to arrest anyone who protests." I showed him a picture of Giselle and explained that the Americans would not let me see her. He responded, "I think that it is terrible that the Americans do not allow you to see your daughter. Is this is the way they treat their own people?"

The conversation continued through an interpreter. We saw military vehicles coming in and out of the base. Black Hawk and Apache helicopters flew over our heads following the Tigris River.

I showed the policeman a few more pictures of my daughter. In one of them she is in uniform behind the wheel of a military bus. In another one she is sitting pretty in a big comfy chair in one of Saddam Hussein's former palaces.

"The Americans promise much: democracy, liberty, security. And yet, we have none of those things," continued the captain. "We were better off before. All of us prefer Saddam's times."

The depth of his convictions and his anti-American sentiment make it even more difficult for our military to win the war. He represents ordinary Iraqi people, especially in the Sunni Zone in central Iraq, the favored area of the former regime. I commented, "If this is what people think, we're in a lot of trouble." Joining the conversation, Medea Benjamin interjected, "But you've been liberated from a dictator." Another officer, Mohanan Majeed Taha, responded, "We did not ask for anyone to free us. What gives the Americans the right to liberate us?"

At this point the base spokesperson, Lt. Nathan Carver, approached me. Lt. Carver is a tall, blond, light-eyed, good-looking man in his thirties. He informed me that my daughter would probably be back very late that day or maybe the next day. After explaining how the area becomes very dangerous after five in the afternoon he added, "Ma'am, you can see your daughter tomorrow if, and only if, you come alone. No press." I was so happy I hugged him and thanked him. A few moments later he confided, "If my mother were to do what you're doing, it'd break my heart!" His words filled me with tenderness. I could tell he really wanted to see his mother.

Capt. Hussein offered to take us to the police station and proceeded to invite us to dinner at his home, promising us barbecued lamb. He joked that if the Americans would not let me hug my daughter, at least he would show me true Iraqi hospitality. Capt. Hussein is the one who gave me the rosary I have on my left hand in the picture of me and the Iraqi policemen. I thanked him for the offer, but we had decided it was best if we returned to Baghdad. We were already taking too many risks. Capt. Hussein replied, "I hope your daughter treats our people well, not like some of the Americans. In return, she will be treated well by us and, God willing, she will remain safe."

En route to Tikrit, I witnessed the remains of this American tank

Base spokesman Lt. Nathan Carver hugging me after validating my visit to see my daughter.

Giselle stands up in front of a huge Saddam Hussein Mural.

15

I FIND MY DAUGHTER

Saturday, December 6, 2003. At seven o'clock in the morning I was having breakfast in the dining area, as usual. The press was already there. This was the big day and it was my last opportunity to find my daughter Giselle. The next day we had to return to Jordan.

Our Iraqi driver was ready to go. We were on our way to Tikrit for the second time. On the way we saw some Spanish cameramen filming a documentary. They asked us if we wanted to participate. There was a very large building, most of which had been bombed out by the Americans. It had been raining and we were cold. The people making the documentary found a good place for the interview and soon began asking their questions. I don't remember exactly what they were. I was feeling so many things inside. I felt lethargic, but I don't know if it was because of being so tired or for some other reason. I remember my friends telling me we were on the news in the United States and all over the world. At the time I did not quite understand. I could not imagine what the media were doing since I did not watch television or even read a newspaper. I was living my dream and allowed myself to be led by daily events. I was not fully aware of what was happening because we had to go to so many places everyday. I really didn't have time to process what was going on around us.

Finally, the interview ended and we walked through the building. I thought it must have been a very beautiful and elegant place before the bombs destroyed it. They told us people paid a small fee to live there. Suddenly, we saw children appear. They had no shoes and were not dressed for the weather. We had brought some candy and gave them some. I brought some nutritional chocolate bars along because the day before we had gone without eating most of the day. I did not think twice about giving them to the children. Not all the children got something, so I told them I would send more with the other driver.

After we came back, I ran to my room, grabbed the boxes, and gave them to the driver so he could give them to the children. Whenever I felt hungry, I would remember the children's happiness and think it was well worth suffering a little hunger to make those children happy.

On the way to Tikrit I saw many trucks loaded with building materials and heavy artillery equipment. I thought, "Too bad the trucks aren't loaded with medical supplies for the hospitals that need them!"

The greatest adversities that people endure after a war are hunger, shortages of medicine, and a lack of basic necessities. I had seen lines of cars waiting up to seven hours just to get gas putting everyone in a bad mood. We did not have to worry about gas since, for the right price, you could buy black market gasoline. What irony!

I was dressed like an Iraqi woman, as I had been the day before. I spent some time talking with our driver, my good friend Sam. I had come to like him. He spoke English perfectly. Suddenly, we saw an American tank in flames. It had been hit by a bomb. I became very sad thinking about how many people had died because of the injustice of the bombings going on. Sam tried to calm me down, saying, "Do not cry. This happens every day." I did not hesitate to say, "My daughter frequently drives on roads like this." He immediately apologized. We continued talking, trying to forget the incident.

We arrived in Tikrit and got out of the vehicle. An officer was already waiting for us. He politely told Sam he could not go on base. He would have to wait outside the gate. The officer led me to a small room made of sandbags. The ground was muddy and there were little puddles of water. A female soldier about twenty checked my camera, my purse, and all over my body. It was routine. Two soldiers put me on a Jeep and drove me to Saddam Hussein's palace grounds, now an American military base.

I saw small domes on separate towers, like the ones on mosques. In some of the rooms I noticed beautiful gold-framed mirrors. My daughter tells me there is a beautiful swimming pool, too.

Once inside the palace I was taken through a series of very big storerooms. We entered a room with a picture of Saddam Hussein and another room with two computers. There I was informed that Giselle would be there in ten minutes. I started getting nervous. Soon, I would be able to see my daughter and hug her. I sat and waited. Suddenly, the door opened and I saw Giselle dressed in military fatigues, carrying her rifle. I thought, "She should be carrying a book, not a weapon." I had my camera with me but, as soon as I saw her, I ran up and hugged her. I could not stop kissing her and she could not stop kissing me. She was very thin and her nose was sunburned, but she looked well. She was very happy to see me. She exclaimed, "Oh, Mom, the things you do for me!" I answered, "I would go to the ends of earth to find you."

Among all the tears, laughter, and hugs we started to talk. She asked about her father, her sister, about Antony and Ashley (her nephew and niece), and about the rest of the family. She wanted to know everything. It had been two years and ten months. Distance and time had taken their toll.

During the two hours we spent together two soldiers were always in the next room. I knew they did not speak Spanish, but they were able to understand the expressions of love between a mother and daughter. My daughter told me about one day when she was driving a bus over a bridge in Tikrit. She thought, "Better to drive down the center of the road." It surprised her when a bomb exploded. Then another one went off. "There were four bombs altogether, Mom! I had to drive the bus across the bridge and then pull off the side of the road. Right then, soldiers from my division arrived and captured the Iraqi rebels. The little medal of the Virgin Mary Mama Machú gave me and the blessed scapular you sent just before I left are what saved me." I thought it also must have been the prayers many people had said for us.

Later, Giselle shared another story. "One day I was in a convoy of American trucks and buses on routine maneuvers. There were children on the side of the road asking for candy. They knew the soldiers often gave them sweets. I was driving a bus with another soldier next to me. We saw a child about seven years old get hit by a truck and land on the side of the road. We are forbidden to stop for an accident because if we did, we could be attacked by Iraqis. We ended up parking not far from the child and ran back to him. It was horrible. The child's entire face was bloody. His arms and legs were twisted. My partner took a small towel out of his first aid kit and put it on the child's forehead. I immediately took a defensive position:

pointing my rifle in all directions to cover us in case we were attacked. A few seconds later we saw the child's parents come out screaming and crying. We signaled them to follow us as we put the child in the back of the bus. We left them at a place where they care for the wounded at the edge of town. We never knew what happened to the child."

My daughter asked one of the soldiers in the next room to take some pictures of us. A half-hour later they brought us three plates of food. I was so emotional I could hardly eat. The soldiers were very nice and attentive. They were good people. I now understood it was the press they were bothered by the day before.

What shocked me most about the base was that every night at 9:30 they would sit and wait for the mortars the Iraqis would fire into the base. Later, I found out this had happened every day for over six months. The patio was almost completely destroyed, *just like soldiers' minds are when they return from war.*

It is very important for soldiers far away in a war zone to have frequent contact with their families. It gives them joy and motivates them to carry on. It is something positive for them during the hard times they are going through. Perhaps it may prevent some soldiers from committing suicide in their wild desperation of thinking their families have forgotten them.

Soldiers who return from war should be required

by law to undergo therapy. No matter how strong the person, it is impossible to erase the terror one witnesses during war. The horror felt after combat is realizing you have killed innocent children. If counseling is not given soon, there is a tendency towards divorce, violence, and, in the worst cases, suicide.

The two hours the military gave me with my daughter flew by. It was time to part. Giselle told her comrades I was leaving. As I left the room a friend of my daughter came up to meet me. We went out to the patio where the Jeep was waiting to take me to the gate. Sam would be waiting, too.

We hugged. I gave Giselle my blessing and told her to take care of herself and that we would be waiting for her and her brother. I remember she followed us, walking on the narrow sidewalk with her rifle hanging from her shoulder, waving goodbye. I kept waving, too, until I lost sight of her and quietly started crying.

The soldier who was sitting in the front passenger seat told me, "Ma'am, your daughter's going to be alright. Don't worry. She is well taken care of." I thanked him for his gentle words. We got to the gate and he walked me to where Sam was waiting. I thanked the soldier again and noticed his attitude was firm, hard, without emotion. At that moment I understood this is the way soldiers have to be all the time. Underneath, I could see the great human quality in them all.

My daughter as I found her,
moments after being reunited.

My moment of glory when I could finally hug my daughter at her base in Tikrit.

16

RETURN TO BAGHDAD

Our trip back to Baghdad was without incident. We arrived at about five in the afternoon. Sam invited me to see where he and his family lived. It was in the central part of Baghdad. The streets were very narrow and the buildings had several stories.

Sam then took me to the entrance of a dwelling where I saw some children playing. He parked the car at the corner. There were several men there. Some were standing around. Others were sitting at a table. He introduced us. They offered me a cup of tea, a sign of welcome. Later, we took some pictures and said goodbye to them.

Medea and Aman, our interpreter, were at the hotel when I got there. They were very happy to find out I finally got to see my daughter. I told them I wanted to buy some gifts since we were leaving the next day. We went downtown and found several stalls selling fruit and souvenirs. We bought some souvenirs and returned to the hotel where the rest of the group was waiting.

Aman is an intelligent and hard-working Iraqi woman. She was our interpreter during most of our meetings and activities. She was often accompanied by her husband, a teacher and excellent father.

Aman and her family invited us to her home for a farewell party. It was an unforgettable evening. Our good friend Aman, her husband, and their daughters had prepared a delicious meal.

Allow me to share a few anecdotes. When we finally got to the sixth floor, our tongues hanging out from the climb, Aman introduced us to her two precious daughters. Medea gave them a few gifts, among which were some embroidered shawls. They absolutely loved them.

Our friends took out the Iraqi dresses they had bought and started modeling them. We took a lot of pictures. There was Middle Eastern music and everyone started dancing.

Shortly after we got there one of the daughters made a comment that was quite hurtful to me. We had been talking about the troops stationed in the city when the young girl said, "I hate the American uniforms." I was very offended by the comment. I thought of my children and the thousands of soldiers who had given their lives so that the Iraqi people could have a better life. I thought of all the human lives lost during this stupid war, as pop star Ricky Martin once said. This is a war about power and ambition and the lengths people will go to in order to meet those goals. I mentioned the incident to one of the group members. For a moment I felt I should leave the party, but it soon became quite lively and the incident was forgotten.

At dinner time they stared bringing large trays of food: chicken, lamb rolls, fruit salads, and a wide variety of dishes and beverages. Finally, it was time to say goodbye and each of us said a few words of thanks. When it was my turn I said I was very happy to be in this marvelous land and thanked them for their kind hospitality. At the same time I felt sad that I was leaving my two loved ones behind. You can imagine the rest. I could not continue. Tears rolled from my eyes and my words of farewell came to an end.

We left the party at about ten o'clock. Some of the members of the group and I walked through the streets of Baghdad to the Palestine Hotel. In the lobby we found out there was an art exhibition. We roamed around a little and then went straight to use the computer room, very excited about our last night in this faraway land. Very early the next morning we would leave for Amman. We left the Palestine Hotel and started walking the streets. It was eleven o'clock. There was no one outside and it was very dark. We were talking and laughing about everything when somebody said, "Where's the terrorism?" We said the same thing, "Where's the terrorism?"

To this day I often think about how lucky we were. God, along with the prayers of so many people, was always with us. It was an unforgettable trip, forever etched in our hearts.

Sam and I sharing tea with neighbors in Baghdad

Enjoying tea with Sam and his friends, in his neigborhood in Baghdad

17

GOODBYE TO BAGHDAD

We left the Hotel Agadir at about nine o'clock in the morning, saying our goodbyes to the people who had opened their hearts to us and who had organized all the activities we were involved in. We slowly left the hotel behind.

We made our way through the streets of this beautiful city. We ended up on a four-lane highway. We passed a convoy of American tanks on our right. The young men were pointing their M16s, somewhat tense, tired, looking very seriously all around them. Excitedly we stuck our heads out the window and yelled, "Hello boys! We're Americans, too! We're all waiting for you to come home. We're very proud of you." They turned their heads looking quite surprised and started teasing each other. A couple of them waved. We were very happy to see them. I kept desperately looking for my son Chuveny. It was impossible. All the soldiers looked alike in their uniforms. Up until then I had kept my word not to look for my son, as he had asked me. My mother's heart ached at the thought of leaving my two children in this hell, not knowing if they would return alive or dead. Nevertheless, at the bottom of my heart I felt they would return safe and sound.

We could not continue with our expressions of happiness. The driver warned us what we were doing was very dangerous. Iraqi rebels would attack at any moment. We quieted down and sat back taking everything in.

At about five o'clock in the afternoon we arrived at a small town. We stopped to rest and went into a restaurant full of Iraqi men. They stared at us as if we were strange animals. We did not know what was going on. Our driver said they would not serve us until we went to the other room with all the other women. Medea refused, saying we wanted to eat at the same table and to please serve us. We all sat down and shared a table with the Iraqi men.

Some of the men ate very carefully. They had neither silverware nor napkins, used something like a thick tortilla to eat with, and quite contentedly licked their fingers. Some of them were tall and light-skinned with handsome, manly features. Others were dark, thin, and not so good looking. Many of them resembled my own Mexican people.

When we arrived at the Jordanian border we found an endless line of cars waiting to cross. It was going to take several hours and we might miss our flight. Medea and Fernando gathered our passports and tickets and went to talk to the person in charge. I took advantage of the situation to look for a restroom. I walked about a block and found one. I was surprised to see there were no toilets, only small stalls with doors and a hole in the middle of the floor. Forget about toilet paper! There was just a small hose to wash up with afterwards. The floor was so wet I had to raise the bottoms of my pant legs. I went practically standing up. The conditions were very unsanitary. I wanted to wash my hands, but there was no soap, let alone paper to dry my hands with. It reminded me of when my husband and I were in Belgrade, Serbia. There, I paid to use the bathroom in a restaurant and still there were only holes in the floor. So, it was not much of a surprise to find this in Iraq, too.

When I got back, my friends were already worrying about me. My God! Even though we were in the midst of so much danger, nothing had happened to us. I thank God for all the people who were constantly praying for our well-being. Finally, Medea and Fernando had arranged for us to cross the border. The guards opened a lane to the left so our two vehicles could pass. The waiting Iraqis got angry and started honking their horns in protest. We waved at them through our open windows.

We arrived in Amman with time to spare. We made our flight to Amsterdam.

18

MILITARY RECRUITMENT

Military recruitment of young people in American high schools is a nefarious scheme. Military recruiters start brainwashing our children from a very young age. They make false promises and deliberately deceive the young people. Their only purpose is to send soldiers to Iraq, Afghanistan, or any other place cannon fodder is needed.

We all know about the benefits offered by a military career. Young people have opportunities to advance their human development, to receive technical or college educations, and to become good future citizens. However, quite often they have to make the ultimate sacrifice, shedding their blood for their country.

Life is the most valuable thing human beings have. Those who believe the contrary are not thinking clearly. They do not have both feet on the ground. What is worse is they do not have God in their hearts. They feel empty and sad, not able to see the true light. A lot of young people are involved in gangs. I wonder, "Why don't the recruiters approach the kids in gangs and recruit them, get them to shape up. Why don't they educate them, offer them a chance at a better life?

Similarly, there are over two million inmates in the United States' prison system. Why not enlist these young men, train them, and send them to war?

High school students are not mature enough to make decisions and good judgments about what they want to do with their lives. Nevertheless, the high school your son or daughter goes to is very likely giving out personal information to recruiting officers without your permission, allowing your child to be subject to military recruitment.

The legal justification for it all is the infamous "No Child Left Behind" act. This law includes a provision that high schools throughout the nation provide the Department of Defense with a listing of the names, addresses, and telephone numbers of all 11th and 12th graders, or else risk losing federal funds.

Before this provision went into effect, a third of all U.S. high schools refused petitions from recruiters and denied them access to campuses. They did not believe it was an appropriate way to go about things. Now, all schools assist the Pentagon in its search for young people, making the students feel obligated to enter this dangerous and violent profession.

Recently, Sunnyside Unified School District in Tucson, Arizona modified its regulations, limiting the number of visits by military and other recruiters to one visit per month. The high school's principal has the option to adjust the number of visits allowing for special circumstances. Enrollment materials now include a form for parents to fill out, permitting or not permitting the disclosure of the student's information to military recruiters.

19

SEXUAL HARASSMENT IN THE MILITARY

I am a mother like thousands and thousands of others who only want the best for their children. We, as mothers, want to believe the world is filled with good people. We want our children to be protected from bad things while in the armed forces. However, we are sadly mistaken. Women in the military suffer constant sexual harassment from their fellow soldiers and even from some of their superior officers.

We must not lose sight of the danger women soldiers face everyday. There are people within the military who abuse their power and position in order to satiate their base instincts.

This is a warning to all parents who want their children to enlist in the army to be aware of this travesty. It is something their children will have to face once they join up.

My daughter used to call from Tikrit and tell me about the constant harassment she endured from one of her commanders. She even confided that once, back in Texas, she filed a complaint that was swept under the rug.

The authorities feel compelled to hide scandals in order to preserve the honor of the armed forces. Instead, they should select personnel rigorously and integrate current research about sexual abuse. Courts-martial within the military ought to be fairer, immediately sanctioning the guilty parties.

20

STORY OF AN UNCERTAIN DEATH

This is a true story. Like thousands more that often end unsolved, the story of this family ends in the desolation, frustration, and pain that ensue when, fighting against the impotence we feel when our loved ones die, we are given information that is untrue.

Such is the case of Juan Torres, 27, stationed in Afghanistan, serving his country, and happy that in two weeks he would be going home to his loved ones and friends.

He often called home saying how he saw many things that did not seem right in the armed forces, including drug abuse.

Two weeks before Juan was to leave his family received a notice saying Juan committed suicide. The entire family was devastated. Only after his burial did they find out Juan's death had not been suicide, but an act of treachery. This is why his battalion was told to say the contrary.

Deaths like Juan Torres's often go unexplained. They continue to happen over and over again, violating the human rights of the innocent victims, their friends, and their families.

May Juan Torres rest in peace.

21

WASHINGTON, D.C.

Our arrival in Washington was truly unforgettable. The airport was covered with a white sheet of snow. Our challenging mission accomplished, we felt very happy. We returned from Iraq triumphant. We thought the information we brought back might be of value to many people, including our congressmen and the President himself.

The day after our arrival we went to the Capitol. A press conference had been arranged. My cell phone would not stop ringing. Several reporters wanted to interview me, Fernando, and the rest of the group. A radio personality wanted to interview me live from a telephone booth in the Capitol. In the interview, called "A Mother's Christmas Gift," I told the interviewer this was my Christmas present: the two joyful hours I spent with my daughter Giselle.

We went into a room where the national press had gathered. A congressional representative informed us that because of the holidays the congressmen were not available. This made us feel like the information we brought from Iraq was not important to them. However, thanks to the media, our message and our demands were made public – every single word. A reporter asked me, "Mrs. Valencia, what message would you like to send to President Bush?" I replied, "Mr. President, it's time to bring the troops home. I want my children to come back alive, not dead." I raised my voice and said, "I want my children to come back alive, not as dead heroes. Thank you."

We felt satisfaction. The message we brought back from Iraq had been given and our search for peace would continue.

22

NEW YORK

After that busy and productive day in Washington, we drove to New York City. We arrived at two in the morning.

Our reasons for going to New York involved a series of activities planned in the city, including visits to the United Nations, meetings at different places, and English and Spanish interviews with the press.

In New York I had the pleasure of making the acquaintance of Camilo Mejia, a Nicaraguan-American soldier. Camilo was the first Iraq War veteran publicly to refuse to serve in the farce happening in Iraq. His request to be discharged as a conscientious objector was rejected at his court-martial. He was found guilty of desertion and sentenced to one year imprisonment at Fort Sill, Oklahoma. Camilo was released February 15, 2005.

Camilo was courageous enough to say, "I will not return to Iraq. I will not contribute to innocent people's deaths. No more blood for oil!"

Camilo is hero to us, and will continue to be so.

We had several interviews with people at the United Nations. One of them was with Mr. Adolfo Aguilar Zinser, the Mexican ambassador. He shared his great enthusiasm on behalf of the Mexican people that there be an end to this war.

Aguilar Zinser was a Mexican leftist. He graduated with a law degree from the Universidad Nacional Autonoma de Mexico and has an International Relations degree from the Colegio de Mexico. In 1978 he received his master's degree in Public Administration from Harvard.

During President Vicente Fox's administration, he acted as Presidential Counsel for National Security (2000-2002) and the Mexican ambassador to the United Nations (2002-2003). After declaring Mexico was the backyard of the United States, he stepped down from his post and went into news reporting. He died in a car accident near Mexico City on June 5, 2005. May he rest in peace.

The next day, Univision television invited me to their studios for an interview, thanks to Angelica Atondo. They wanted to know what had happened in Iraq and asked a lot of questions about my experiences with the Iraqi people. They treated me very nicely and I felt right at home.

Visiting New York was an unforgettable experience. I will always remember that December 15th, walking down Fifth Avenue along with thousands of others, the storefronts all lit up for the holidays. We went to Times Square and to the Statue of Liberty, where we took lots of pictures. We also went to Central Park. It was extremely cold, but that did not keep us from admiring its natural beauty.

Greeted by my husband, grandson and supporters at Tucson International Airport after returning from Iraq.

EPILOGUE

We Americans, along with the entire world, witnessed the attack on September 11, 2001. We were paralyzed with fear. President Bush's bellicose speech would not wait. It reverberated around the world.

Americans and people all over the world protested against that speech and have been protesting our military intervention in Iraq ever since. The people of the United States are once again experiencing the "Vietnam Syndrome."

Was it possible those in the current administration were so stubborn they could not hear the people's message? Or were they deliberately dismissing it and turning a deaf ear to the voices of the people? Either way, they did what they wanted.

By March 20, 2003, the invasion of Iraq had started – without the support of the United Nations, without a declaration of war from United States Congress, and, what is most important, without the consent of the American people.

Over the course of history, people the world over

have suffered and will continue to suffer during wars. Wars have been inflicted upon people for countless millennia.

I understand that some wars have brought about liberty and justice. But they are few and far between.

I pray this situation may reach a positive solution. However, I will never agree with the use of extreme force to resolve conflicts.

I believe that this war should be like the suffering and pain a mother feels when she is about to give birth. Giving birth does not happen without pain. However, the pain is soon replaced with joy and with the tremendous responsibility that bringing a new life into the world entails. The war should be like that: ended soon and with responsibility taken.

If what is happening is the agenda of liars and evil men with evil intentions, then the war in Iraq can very well be compared to childbirth. A new Iraq is being born – one with a new democratic political framework, encompassing all aspects of life and bringing forth new ideals. It can be said that Iraq is in the midst of labor pains. The Iraqi people, especially the unprotected classes, will find this new birth a very difficult one.

My Calvary started when my two children were sent to war. For months I heard nothing from them. Today, they are home once again. Chuveny and Giselle served honorably for five years and are now trying to reenter society, continuing their studies, and getting on with their lives.

In my heart I feel this could very well happen with the Iraqi people, too, even though they continue with their unending Calvary, trying to reconstruct their lives and adjust to a new social contract.

It took only one man to decide to make war on the innocent people of Iraq. I am only one mother who wants to give some love and hope to the most innocent of that country, the children of Iraq.

For more information, or just to get in touch with me, my e-mail address is anabelle1227@yahoo.com or, you can visit my website at www.anabellevalencia.com.

NOTE: A substantial part of the income generated by this book is destined for No More Victims, a non-profit organization helping to find a cure for a type of children's leukemia caused by uranium left over from the first Gulf war.

ACKNOWLEDGEMENTS

The days went on and on. It seemed an eternity for me and my family. Many people we knew and many we didn't called to offer their emotional and spiritual support.

From the bottom of my heart I would like to thank all those friends, teachers, coworkers, priests, and families who were by our side at all times, with special thanks to Mrs. Kinard for the hour she gave me to pray for the people of Iraq.

I would like to thank my husband for his support during the past ten months while I was preparing this book and for the time he spent correcting the original manuscript. I would also like to thank my beloved parents for giving me life and, especially, my mother for believing in me and encouraging me to continue with this crazy idea of contributing at least a grain of sand towards the benefit of those Iraqi children stricken with leukemia. I give thanks to God for protecting my children's lives during this war.

I would like to thank my sister María Antonieta, who was there for me with advice and prayers. I would also like to thank my friend Jorge Ruiz for his valuable ideas, for his thoughts regarding the naming the book *Tears in Iraq*, and for his extraordinary sense of humor. Thanks also to the Peace Activists' Coalition in Tucson, Arizona who were there for me during the toughest times, offered valued support, and, without knowing me directly, sent financial donations to pay for my trip, along with gifts and poems. I would also like to thank Mr. Rick Lipinski for his great help in the revision of the English version.

To all of you, my eternal thanks. May God bless you always.

Congress of the United States

Washington, DC 20515

November 6, 2003

Lt. General Ricardo Sanchez
Commanding General
CJTF-7
Unit 91400
APO AE 09302-1400

Dear General Sanchez:

We are writing on behalf of a group of parents and families of American troops currently serving in Iraq who will be traveling to Iraq at the end of November on a goodwill mission to the Iraqi people and to deliver a message of support to their children and other troops. The delegation will be traveling to Iraq from November 29 to December 8, 2003.

We respectfully ask that you give fair consideration to their request for access to civilian and military installations so they may be able to carry out their mission.

Specifically, the families hope to accomplish three objectives. First, they hope to deliver a message of peace and friendship to the Iraqi people, particularly the children, through letters that American students have written to their Iraqi counterparts. Second, they would like to meet with Ambassador Bremer to discuss and better understand what is happening in Iraq. Finally, the families would like to meet with you in order to personally deliver a message of support and hope from military parents and families to their loved ones serving in Iraq.

The delegation will be led by Mr. Fernando Suarez del Solar, father of U.S. Marine Lance Cpl. Jesus Alberto Suarez del Solar who was killed in action in Iraq on March 27, 2003. Jesus was one of our proud immigrant soldiers, many of whom have been granted United States citizenship posthumously. His story, which is not unlike the story of hundreds of others of our brave young men and women who have served and are serving on behalf of their nation, has touched us deeply. We hope that you will honor their commitment to the nation by doing everything feasible to facilitate the mission of this group of parents and family members to accomplish their objectives.

For more information about the delegation, you may contact Mr. Suarez at (760) 233-0630 or via Ms. Medea Benjamin with Global Exchange, a non-governmental organization that is helping coordinate the trip at (415) 235-6517.

We thank you for your consideration.

Sincerely,

XAVIER BECERRA
Member of Congress

BOB FILNER
Member of Congress

Lt. General Ricardo Sanchez
November 6, 2003
Page 2

SUSAN DAVIS
Member of Congress

HILDA SOLIS
Member of Congress

MAXINE WATERS
Member of Congress

RAUL GRIJALVA
Member of Congress

GRACE F. NAPOLITANO
Member of Congress

DEPARTMENT OF THE ARMY
HEADQUARTERS III CORPS AND FORT HOOD
18010 Hood Road
FORT HOOD, TEXAS 76544-5016

October 19, 2004

REPLY TO
ATTENTION OF

Office of the Installation
Adjutant General

Ms. Anabelle Valencia
1651 West Colonial Heights
Tucson, Arizona 85746

Dear Ms. Valencia:

Thank you for your letter to President George W. Bush concerning your daughter, Sergeant Giselle Valencia. Due to mail screening procedures, we have only recently received your letter. We appreciate your patience in awaiting this response.

Military service is a career like no other. It requires sacrifice on the part of both Soldiers and their families. We understand the difficulties and hardships families endure during long deployments. However, Soldiers receive great satisfaction from helping to accomplish the mission and making the United States a safe and secure place to live. We all owe a debt of gratitude to our dedicated Soldiers. I am sure you are pleased that your daughter returned safely to Fort Hood in March 2004. You can be proud of her military service.

We are glad to be of assistance and hope this information is helpful.

Sincerely,

Charles E. Green, Sr.
Installation Adjutant General

DEPARTMENT OF THE ARMY
HEADQUARTERS, XVIII AIRBORNE CORPS AND FORT BRAGG
FORT BRAGG, NORTH CAROLINA 28310

November 3, 2004

REPLY TO ATTENTION OF

Office of Congressional Liaison

Ms. Anabelle Valencia
1651 W. Colonial Heights
Tucson, Arizona 85746

Dear Ms. Valencia,

This is in response to your recent letter to President George W. Bush, concerning your son, Sergeant Chuveny Valencia, a member of the 82nd Airborne Division, Fort Bragg, North Carolin

Your son safely returned with his unit from Operation Iraqi Freedom in February 2003 and continues to serve this country with honor. Sergeant Valencia's commander reports that your son enlistment will be complete in April 2005, at which time he plans to leave the United States Army

Thank you for your interest in this matter. I hope this information was of assistance to you.

Sincerely,

Joyce H. Thomas

Joyce H. Thomas
Congressional Liaison

JOHN McCAIN
ARIZONA

CHAIRMAN
COMMITTEE ON COMMERCE,
SCIENCE, AND TRANSPORTATION

COMMITTEE ON ARMED SERVICES

COMMITTEE ON INDIAN AFFAIRS

United States Senate

241 Russell Senate Office Building
Washington, DC 20510-0303
(202) 224-2235

4450 South Rural Road
Suite B-130
Tempe, AZ 85282
(480) 897-6289

7400 East Arizona
Biltmore Circle
Suite 1150
Phoenix, AZ 85016
(602) 952-2410

450 West Paseo Redondo
Suite 200
Tucson, AZ 85701
(520) 670-6334

Telephone for Hearing Impaired
(202) 224-7132
(602) 952-0170

September 22, 2003

Anabelle Valencia
1651 W. Colonial Hts.
Tucson, AZ 85746-1356

Dear Anabelle:

Thank you for contacting my office regarding your troubles with your children in Iraq.

Due to provisions of the Privacy Act of 1974, all Federal agencies are prohibited from releasing any information regarding an individual without that individual's written consent. This protection means that I am unable to help until I have something in writing from the person concerned to show that I am authorized to check into the matter. Therefore, I am returning your material to you.

Sincerely,

John McCain

John McCain
United States Senator

JM/tnl
Enclosure(s)

PRINTED ON RECYCLED PAPER

ISBN 142510566-1

9 781425 105662

Edwards Brothers Malloy
Ann Arbor MI. USA
April 24, 2017

'VANILLA OCEANICS' IN THE FITZPATRICK–LELAND HOUSE: VANILLIN, CALONE AND FLOWERPOOL® IN THE HOLLYWOOD HILLS

MARC VOM ENDE AND PHILIP KRAFT

The truth is so boring
We all have each other
Once you were beautiful
Now I am myself
We all had each other
Everything ends in perfume

Soulwax, 'The Truth is so Boring'[1]

Everything ends in perfume. The phrase refers to the way that prayers are sent to heaven at funerals in the form of clouds of myrrh and frankincense. *Per Fumum*—by means of smoke, through nebulization, via the transformation of a substance into something airborne.[2] Incense became a necessity very early on: as an antiseptic that served for deodorising when corpses were disposed of by burning. In this way, scents became a part of religious ceremonies long before they became vectors for private and intimate pleasures.[3] In this way they defined certain architectural areas as sacred, others as unholy, some private, some public, just as soundwaves occupy space and lend it structure and depth via the reflecting walls. Scent and sound give space its atmosphere, its texture, its context. Scents and sounds bring orientation to an otherwise empty space. Thereby, they create subspaces, and in doing so may either mutually and symbiotically reinforce or attenuate one another. Sometimes in the best way, as intended in the exhibition *Resynthesizers*, where the synthetic sounds of Florian Hecker create a dynamic space in the Fitzpatrick–Leland House that becomes a focal point for the olfactory experience, and vice versa. Scent is in the house, so to speak.

As Andy Warhol wrote:

> Empty space is never-wasted space... [A] way to take up more space is with perfume. I really love wearing perfume... When I am walking around in New York I'm always aware of the smells around me: the rubber mats in office buildings; upholstered seats in movie theaters; pizza; Orange Julius; espresso–garlic–oregano; burgers; dry cotton tee-shirts; neighborhood grocery stores; chic grocery stores; the hot dogs and sauerkraut carts; hardware store smell; stationery store smell; souvlaki; the leather and rugs at Dunhill, Mark Cross, Gucci; the Moroccan-tanned leather on the street racks; new magazines, back-issue magazines; typewriter stores; Chinese import stores (the mildew from the freighter); India import stores; Japanese import stores; record stores; health food stores; soda-fountain drugstores; cut-rate drugstores; barber shops; beauty parlors; delicatessens; lumber yards; the wood chairs and tables in the N.Y. Public Library; the donuts,

> pretzels, gum, and grape soda in the subways; kitchen appliance departments; photo labs; shoe stores; bicycle stores; the paper and printing inks in Scribner's, Brentano's, Doubleday's, Rizzoli, Marboro, Bookmasters, Barnes & Noble; shoe-shine stands; grease-batter; hair pomade; the good cheap candy smell in the front of Woolworth's and the dry-goods smell in the back; the horses by the Plaza Hotel; bus and truck exhaust; architects' blueprints; cumin, fenugreek, soy sauce, cinnamon; fried platanos; the train tracks in Grand Central Station; the banana smell of dry cleaners; exhausts from apartment house laundry rooms; East Side bars (creams); Westside bars (sweat); newspaper stands; record stores; fruit stands in all the different seasons—strawberry, watermelon, plum, peach, kiwi, cherry, Concord grape, tangerine, murcot, pineapple, apple—and I love the way the smell of each fruit gets into the rough wood of the crates and into the tissue-paper wrappings.[4]

But do we need such visual clues to become attentive to smells, do we need these clues to be able to contemplate scents? Some modern art historians think so,[5] while more traditional ones do not even recognize olfactory art as a subject for art history. If room fragrances and the scents of objects are to replace actual materials or their absence, then visual clues certainly help to make the connection; yet, if one wants to experience an odoriferous material or a monolithic accord in all its fragrant purity, other clues such as acoustic or tactile ones are more appropriate, since they are more abstract. In this way, the acoustic spaces of Hecker's work can direct and sharpen yet also disorient and challenge the senses, creating a situation where the odors unfold their sculptural presence, thereby interacting not only with one another but also with the sonic architecture of the Fitzpatrick–Leland House, designed by Rudolf Schindler (1887–1953), one of the most seminal modern architects, famous for his concrete radicalism. Schindler's buildings are ideal venues for olfactory and sonic art as he is the prototypical space architect: 'I consider myself the first and still one of the few architects who consciously abandoned stylistic sculptural architecture in order to develop space as a medium of art.'[6] In *Resynthesizers*, the space of the Fitzpatrick–Leland House is the medium for art, sound and scent become sculptural elements. Odors and sounds provide the atmosphere for the architectural space, and atmosphere creates emotions.

In architecture, perfume and scent is almost never considered or included in teaching.[7] Although in architecture as in perfumery natural components are combined with synthetic products and advanced materials, smell is almost never the criterion for the selection of buiding materials, except for the precious hinoki wood in Japan with its characteristic aroma. Architecture is overly concerned with how buildings are *seen*, whereas smell usually has negative connotations, since historically, bad smells were linked to decay and disease.[8] This led to constructing spaces that were as open as possible, and we find this well demonstrated in the conception of the Fitzpatrick–Leland House. Unintentionally, but very favorably for the enjoyment of olfactory art and contemplation of it,[9] these open spaces allow scents *to breathe*, to diffuse freely and interact with one another, making possible a greater awareness of their common aspects or dissonant facets.

In response to *Resynthesizers*, three olfactory-art accords were devised, each based around one key perfumery material. These are diffused at three discrete locations throughout the building. They explore the intersecting odor space between three significant milestones in Fragrance Chemistry dating from 1874, 1966 and 2021 respectively—thereby connecting to references in some of Hecker's recent works, which reappear in further abstracted or highly progressed modalities within *Resynthesizers*, where the libretto by Robin Mackay[10] and the sound synthesis algorithm by Axel Röbel[11] refer to previous projects such as *FAVN* (2016), *Resynthese FAVN* (2017), and *Inspection II* (2019).

When you encounter an olfactory sensation, you may want to analyze and characterize it even before identifying it as vanillic or marine, and you may want to relate it also to the other sensations surrounding it. In analogy to the *Principles of Art History* (1915) by Heinrich Wölfflin, one could classify odor impression in terms of five opposing pairs:[12] (A) Pyramidal/Monolithic: Does the scent possess a block-like construction as opposed to a sharp, pyramidal evaporation curve? (B) Voluminous/Contrasty: Are common odor aspects adding to a comprehensive whole, or does the character significantly stem from contrasting olfactory impressions? (C) Diffusive/Substantive: Is the scent room-filling or does it cling to the walls and ceiling? (D) Light/Dark: Does the scent appear as luminous, bright, and sunny, or is it dark, dim, dull or smoky? (E) Transparent/Opaque: Is the scent transparent with all elements shimmering through the top, or is it matte and opaque in appeal? These qualities are largely independent of the odor character or its odor family, but make us aware of the structure and composition technique of a scent, or the way in which scents mix and interact. The next step is of course to associate the sensory impressions with known odor impressions from familiar materials or scenes, but it is specifically this scent appearance that correlates with sounds, as we can describe both with similar adjectives although apparently unrelated 'at first sight'.

Everything ends in perfume, but everything begins in perfume as well, when we smell the vanillin (**1**) in breast milk for the very first time,[13] its sweetness enhanced by Furaneol (**2**), the buttery note of diacetyl (**3**) and the honey character of phenylacetic acid (**4**). In this way, nature provides us as babies with a sort of vanilla milkshake plus honey, the creaminess of which is further enhanced by the fruity-floral coconut character of γ-nonalactone (**5**) and the milky-creamy santal effect of such steroids as 5α-androst-16-en-3α-ol (**6**). Yet, whatever else might contribute, vanillin (**1**) is key. Vanillin (**1**) is the primal perfumery material, *der Urduft*, universally loved from early childhood for its aura of well-being and untainted happiness.[14] The elucidation of its structure by Ferdinand Tiemann (1848–1899) and Wilhelm Haarmann (1847–1931) marks the beginning of Fragrance Chemistry. In 1874, Haarmann and Tiemann synthesized vanillin (**1**) from the coniferin contained in pinewood sap by hydrolysis of the β-D-glucopyranoside with the enzyme emulsin.[15] The year 1875 saw the founding of the industrial plant Haarmann's Vanillinfabrik (the predecessor of Symrise), and in 1876 the newly discovered Reimer–Tiemann reaction, along with its inventor Karl Reimer, was integrated, making it Haarmann & Reimer. Thus, vanillin (**1**) corresponds in time with Stéphane Mallarmé's poem 'L'après-midi d'un faune'. Vanillin (**1**) is a sort of resynthesis of vanilla extract achieved by focusing only on its primary active smelling principle, and is therefore more vanilla than vanilla—a supernatural vanilla. It was famously used by Aimé Guerlain in *Jicky* (Guerlain, 1889), is a part of the *Guerlinade* (vanillin, coumarin, orris, rose and jasmine) also prominent in *Shalimar* (Guerlain, 1925) by Jacques '*Jicky*' Guerlain, and basically constitutes, together with ambery materials, the foundation of the 'Oriental' family of perfumes.

Calone 1951 (**7**, 7-methyl-2*H*-benzo[*b*][1,4]dioxepin-3(4*H*)-one), quite contrary to vanillin (**1**), does not occur in nature, though it does perfectly recall the marine note of the ocean. In addition, it also features the characteristic fruity aroma of watermelons; hence, compound **7** is also known as watermelon ketone, and hence watermelons recall water though, as mentioned, Calone 1951 (**7**) is not a constituent of natural watermelon flavor. It thus can be understood as an abstract 'force of nature', and established the aquatic-marine family of scents. What started in the late 1980s as an aquatic nuanceur to muguet accords would go on to develop into an epitome of the 1990s and early 2000s. The trendsetters were *New West for Her* (Aramis, 1990) by Yves Tanguy and *Escape* (Calvin Klein, 1991) by Jean-Marie Santontoni. Calone 1951 (**7**) was prominently mentioned as an ingredient in *Hugo Element* (Hugo Boss, 2009) and in *fluo_ral* (Nomenclature, 2019), both by Nathalie Feisthauer. There is even a home fragrance called simply *Calone 17* (Le Labo, 2015), and in *Replica Beach Walk* (Maison Martin Margiela, 2012) by Jacques Cavallier and Marie Salamagne, Calone 1951 (**7**) is featured along with other related benzodioxepinones. Owing to the overdosing of Calone 1951 in many of these products, however, what had once been experienced as fresh and natural would for many become associated with a functional and synthetic scent. In the context of this project, Calone 1951 (**7**), whose seismic repercussions only began to be felt in the late 1980s, might be related to ideas on artificial representation and technological systems that Jean-François Lyotard developed partly while working in Southern California in the late 1970s and early 1980s, and which ultimately found their form in the exhibition *Les Immatériaux* (1985) and Lyotard's notion of 'Immaterials'.[16] But how does Calone 1951 (**7**) relate to vanillin (**1**)?

By serendipity, it was discovered that vinylic Calones such as **8** possessed very low odor thresholds (th) in the range of steroids such as 5α-androst-16-en-3α-ol (**6**), i.e. th 0.000141 ng/L air.[17] This was rationalised with a flattened structure owing to hyperconjugation, which then indicated that the crucial aliphatic hydrophobe must be situated in the plane of the aromatic ring on the respective receptor binding site for optimal fit and odorant activity. The lower homologue **9** is also a very intense marine odorant with a threshold 0.0125 ng/L air, but interestingly possesses unexpected but very prominent sweet-spicy vanilla aspects. These originate from the aldehyde **10**, which is formed by slow oxidative cleavage of the vinylic double bond of **10**. The aldehyde **10** does indeed display a nice sweet-spicy vanilla odor, easily explained by its structural similarity to vanillin (**1**)—just consider the three oxygen functions on the aromatic nucleus. The structural similarities between so-called 'vanilla oceanics' such as **9** and **10** and vanillin (**1**) indicate that there should be a common odor space between vanilla and marine odorants, as otherwise discords would arise in the odor profile of **9** and **10**. These vanilla–marine coherencies are explored in the experimental accords that form serendipitously when vanilla and marine scents meet in the open space of the Fitzpatrick–Leland House.

To fathom out and understand the nature of these accords in an inquisitive and interactive way, a third perfumery raw material comes into play in *Resynthesizers*: The new captive odorant Flowerpool® is a novel high-impact material produced by Symrise with a boosting clean scent that has an unusual effect on white floral and aquatic notes. Here we are in

2021, firmly in the now, with a material whose antiseptic character recalls the smell of Covid-19 antiseptics. This clean-smell booster has an animalic and leathery creosolic scent with earthy-camphoraceous aspects, and if you look at vanillin (**1**) and creosol (4-methyl guaiacol, **11**) you clearly see another structural analogy. Now, what is highly interesting to note is that in higher concentration, an even more antiseptic character is obtained: the effect of bleach, a halogen effect, the smell of iodine in the air at the beach, and even the scent of elemental chlorine. This halogen effect completes the watermelon aquatic freshness of the Calone 1951 (**7**) accord with the realistic, somewhat aggressive spume of the sea, the sea spray that makes us taste sea salt on our tongues. It also recalls the brine and ozone smell of γ-cyclohomogeranyl chloride (**12**), which is formed in the ocean from γ-cyclohomogeranyl acrylaldehyde (**13**) with its typical ambery seawater smell. But before we drift into ambergris, let us smell, study, and enjoy the trialogue of vanillin, Calone 1951 and Flowerpool® for our delight, delectation, and contemplation. The synthetic analog of vanilla signifies the security symbolized in the structured architectural space of the Fitzpatrick–Leland House, while the scents of bracing natural elements featured in Calone 1951 and Flowerpool® suggest an interplay with the lush coastlines of the Pacific and LA's urbanized modern lifestyle—Vanillin, Calone and Flowerpool® in the Hollywood Hills.

EVERYTHING BREATHES PERFUME: Become part of olfactory art!

1 Soulwax, *Any Minute Now* (Play It Again Sam Records, PIASB 060, 2004), track 11.
2 G. Ohloff, W. Pickenhagen, P. Kraft, F. Grau, *Scent and Chemistry: The Molecular World of Odors* (Weinheim: Wiley-VCH, 2022).
3 Ibid.
4 A. Warhol, *The Philosophy of Andy Warhol: From A to B and Back Again* (London: Penguin Books, 2007), 43–53.
5 Excerpt from an e-mail from Prof. Dr. Bettina Gockel, Institute of Art History, University of Zurich, to Dr. Philip Kraft, Tuesday, 30 August 2016: 'Art history is a discipline whose categories can be challenged and altered by contemporary art. Just as, with the "exit from painting [*Ausstieg aus dem Bild*]" in the sixties, installations, performance, etc. emerged as practices which are now wholly recognized as belonging to the subject matter of art history, in the same way, other themes and devices in the arts may become the object of art-historical research, including scent, or rather perfumes, in so far as they are used as a component of artistic practice. [...] Fragrances are an interesting field at a time when room scents and the scents of objects are apparently intended to replace actual scents or their absence. This kind of artificial olfactory backdrop may prove to be a fertile and critical theme for art.'
6 R. M. Schindler to Elisabeth Mock at the Museum of Modern Art (MoMA), August 1943.
7 A. Barbara and A. Perliss, *Invisible Architecture: Experiencing Places through the Sense of Smell* (Milan: Skira, 2006), 98–102.
8 A. Corbin, *The Foul and the Fragrant: Odor and the French Social Imagination* (Cambridge, MA: Harvard University Press, 1988).
9 P. Kraft, 'The Odor Value Concept in the Formal Analysis of Olfactory Art', *Helv. Chim. Acta* 102: 1 (2019), e1800185. DOI: 10.1002/hlca.201800185.
10 R. Mackay, 'Return of the Faun', in F. Hecker, *Formulations*, ed. S. Gaensheimer, M. Wandschneider and R. Mackay (London: Koenig Books, 2016), <http://readthis.wtf/writing/return-of-the-faun-formulations/>.
11 A. Röbel, 'Sound Processing for the Production of *Resynthese FAVN*', in F. Hecker, *Halluzination, Perspektive, Synthese* (Berlin: Sternberg, 2017).
12 Kraft, 'The Odor Value Concept'.
13 A. Buettner, 'A Selective and Sensitive Approach to Characterize Odour-active and Volatile Constituents in Small-scale Human Milk Samples', *Flavour Fragr. J.* 22 (2007), 465–473. DOI: 10.1002/ffj.1822.
14 J. Mensing, *Schöner Riechen. Die magische Wirkung von Parfüms auf das Wohlbefinden* (Berlin: Springer Verlag, 2021), 258.
15 B.B. Kuhse, *Der Herr Der Düfte. Mit Vanille zum Multimillionär* (Holzminden: Jörg Mitzkat, 2014).
16 R. Mackay, 'Immaterials, Exhibition, Acceleration', in Y. Hui and A. Broeckmann (eds.), *30 Years after Les Immatériaux: Art, Science, Theory* (Meson Press, 2015).
17 P. Kraft, K. Popaj, P. Müller, and M. Schär, 'Vanilla Oceanics: Synthesis and Olfactory Properties of (1'*E*)-7-(Prop-1'-enyl)-2H-benzo[*b*][1,4]dioxepin-3(4*H*)-ones and Homologues', *Synthesis* 17 (2010), 3029–3036. DOI: 10.1055/s-0030-1258142.

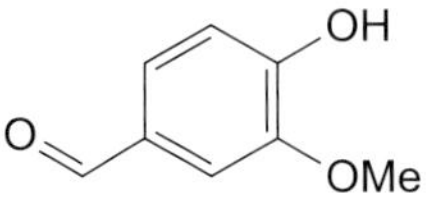

1
vanillin
(1874)

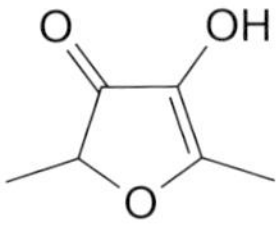

2
Furaneol

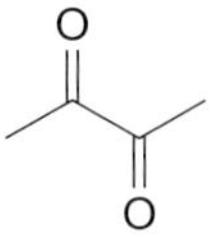

3
diacteyl

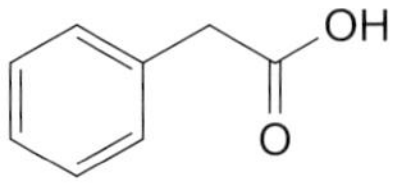

4
phenylacetic acid

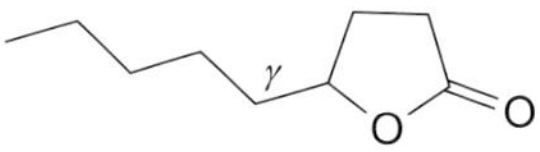

5
γ-nonalactone

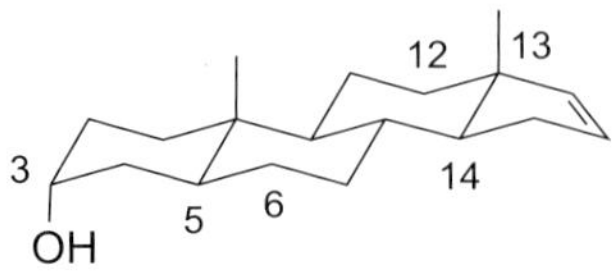

6
α-androst-16-en-3α-ol
th 0.00067 ng/L air

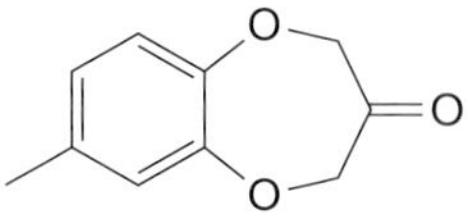

7
Calone 1951
(1966)

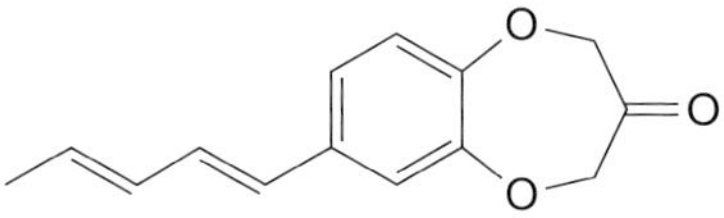

8
green, watery, metallic, aldehydic
th 0.000141 ng/L air

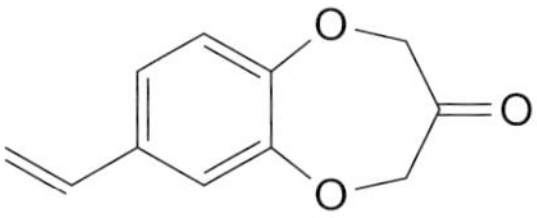

9
marine, green-spicy, vanilla

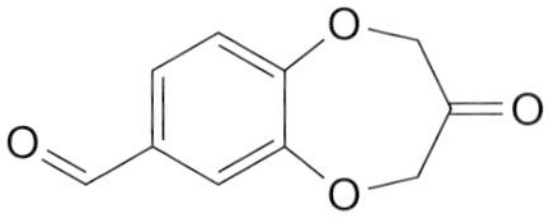

10
sweet, vanilla, spicy

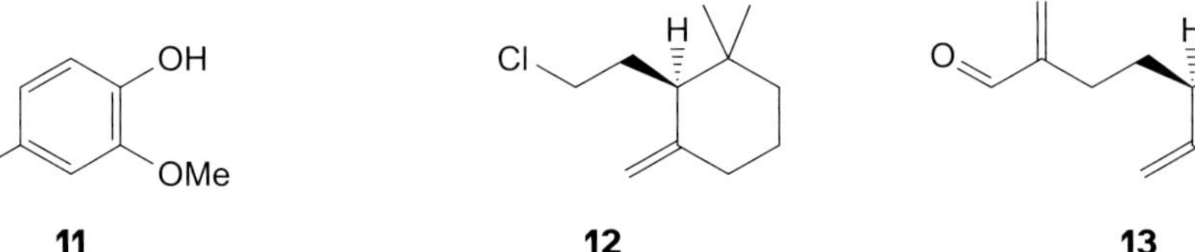

11
creosol

12
γ-cyclohomogeranyl chloride

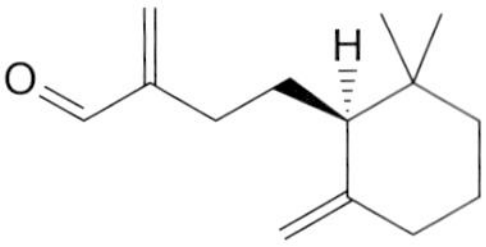

13
γ-cyclohomogeranyl
acrylaldehyde

Vanillin (**1**) and other constituents of breast milk **2–6** as well as Calone 1951 (**7**) and its derivatives **1–10**, creosol (**11**) and ocean-smelling ambergris constituents **12** and **13** with briney, ozonic scents.

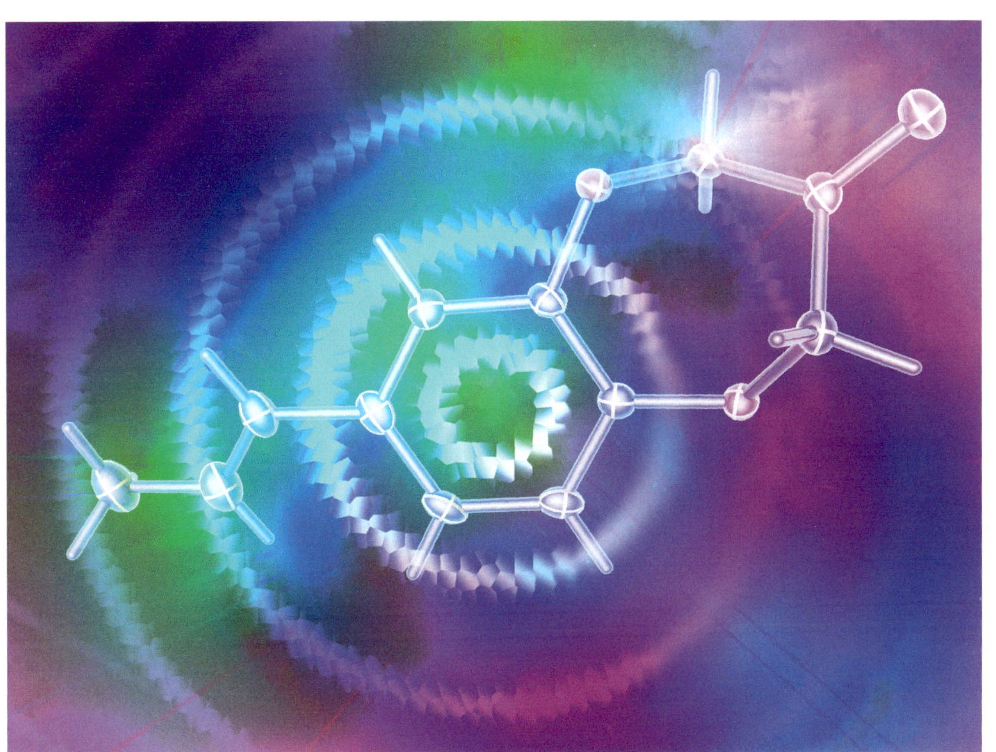

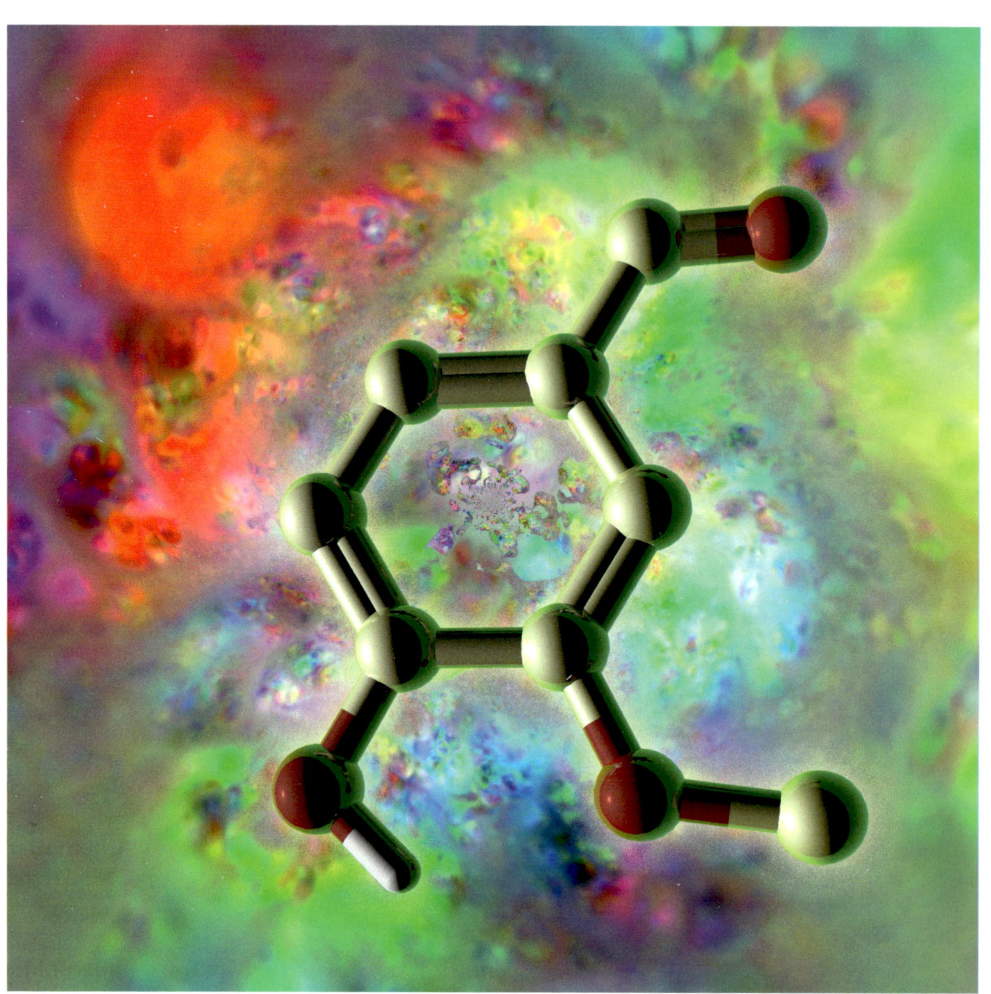

Vanillin (**1**)

15 An artistic representation of Flowerpool®

A DIAUDITORY NOTE ON SYNOPSIS

ROBIN MACKAY

> Synopsis, in Greek, means that one has an overall view of what one plans to do. With this principle of an overall view what is presupposed is that the designer of the exhibition is in a position to bring into view the totality of what he has conceived [...] We can see that the very concept of synopsis poses a problem...[1]

The traditional role played by writing in exhibitions is to assist the visitor, to guide them in their physical journey through the exhibition site and their mental integration of its contents. In an on-site intervention where the visitor has to traverse shifting zones of overlapping auditory, architectural, textual, and olfactory components, this might seem all the more crucial.

Evidently, this role must be refused. Consider Florian Hecker's consistent reference (*A Script for Machine Synthesis* [2015], *Formulations* [2016], *Synopsis* [2017] and *Synopsis Seriation* [2018–2021]) to Jean-François Lyotard's exhibition *Les Immatériaux*, for which the philosopher carefully elaborated an original conceptual schema in response to a technical age in which the materials for both industrial and artistic projects are not just manipulated but increasingly *constituted* by processes describable as 'linguistic'. As Lyotard sensed, this heralded an upheaval in the relation between subject, project, and material, a generalization of coding systems which would unseat natural language from its privileged position in relation to the planning and evaluation of constructive enterprises, whether industrial or artistic.

The auditory and olfactory components put in place by Hecker and his collaborators for *Resynthesizers* conform to Lyotard's description of 'immaterials': they are the output of processes in which materials productive of sensory encounters are subject to fine manipulation by technologically-enabled analyses and machine languages. In the case of *Resynthesizers,* Hecker places the emphasis on the synthetic reconstruction, extension, or extrapolation of existing materials, in the form of auditory texture synthesis and the chemical synthesis of odors.

The overlapping volumes of Rudolph Schindler's Fitzpatrick–Leland House accommodate a set of diffusion systems designed to fill the space with these immaterials. The challenge for the visitor is to integrate the shifting superimpositions of resynthesized sensory components encountered in freely navigating the house. Since these are sensory components abstracted from natural sources and contexts and placed in unfamiliar conjunctions, this challenge tends to be relayed from the level of recognition to that of cognition: the visitor is compelled to make a mental effort at a synopsis to which the work itself provides no clues.

Knowing as much or as little as the artist himself does of how this effort might succeed, or of the potential principles according to which these components might hang together, I have supplemented them with a set of word diffusers. While not refusing the indexical function of language, they are designed to sit alongside rather than above the other subsystems, relaying some of the textual materials that entered into preparations for the project and addressing each of the project's elements (including themselves) in turn.

Words, present here in their most recent technological incarnation, as patterns made and unmade in an electrophoretic display, deferring any synoptic role, are treated as things—that is, as immaterials. With the resynthesis of components drawn from the source materials of this project and its predecessors, the 'libretto' seeks complicity with the operation of the overall assemblage: forcing the reader, interpellated by colliding and incomplete cues, to determine what sense, if any, can be made.

But the figure of the reader itself is also interrogated under the auspices of *Les Immatériaux*'s diagnosis of a radical shift in the subject-project-materials relation.

In his preliminary report on the development of the exhibition, Lyotard lays out a systematic set of oppositions that define the break between modern and postmodern along the axis of the visual and the auditory, the synchronic and the diachronic. On one side he places the formerly hegemonic power of vision, the image, and space, on the other side hearing, language, and time. In the movement from one paradigm to the other, the traditional exhibition, defined as a carefully plotted trajectory through cultural space, will be replaced by a movement with no primary orientation, and a temporalization will come to supersede the spatialization of inscription.

According to Lyotard, drawing on Diderot, the classic itinerary of the exhibition invites the eye of the spectator to a promenade through an inverted city street (the gallery) from which they may gaze out through the 'windows' of paintings onto edifying cultural vistas. The age of immaterials challenges us to work instead with information in motion, only ever partially available. We must acknowledge the impossibility of constructing any such contained and synoptic view of culture, any straight and narrow path to edification.

Presciently, Lyotard goes on to relate this shift to a new mode of reading. The act of reading passes from a visual to an auditory model, given that text is increasingly presented to us not as synoptic pages but as a temporalized inscription in which a text is never actualized all at once. If 'this predominance of time signifies a sort of preeminence of movement over rest', such reading can be said to be 'of the order of hearing':

> In front of their screens, humans—contrary to what we might think—cease to be lookers and become readers—that is to say, essentially, listeners.[2]

The epochal table of distinctions headed by the synchronic and the diachronic, then, also includes two distinct modes of taking in information, keyed respectively to the visual and the auditory:

> [T]he server sends pages to the screen which we read and in which we seek the information we're after. This is an exercise in reading, we read page after page, but this reading, precisely, is not properly speaking a vision, not if we take vision in a strong sense. It is rather of the order of hearing.[3]

To this succession of distinctions, we might add the urban doublet *Paris / LA*, as suggested in the collection of notes entitled *Pacific Wall* which, in a series of strange overcharged theory-fictions attributed to a disappeared rogue academic, reflect on Lyotard's time at the University of California.

The text 'Associate Professors' addresses the mutually profitable exchange of desire involved in the importing of European scholars to the US. Where the 'Romans' want to see in the 'Greeks' their old-world origins, the 'Greeks' are fascinated with the US as a center of power, a new Rome—but are disabused as they realize that this center or capital is in fact a mongrelized, dispersed, contingent and fragmented city ('Rome isn't Rome any more. The USA isn't a country').[4] The contingency of contemporary power under capital deconcentrates the capital: 'there isn't a supreme authority. There's a joining up of surfaces—white, ephemeral, labyrinthine, useless.'[5]

To those Europeans tempted to profit from arriving in the center of the New World as representatives of a cultural origin, Lyotard declares: 'your purpose in coming here should be to lose your culture, to deculturate [...] this center is the true nomad [...] all cultures come here and exchange their movement quantities—lose themselves.'[6]

This idea is reinforced in 'The Labyrinth at the Center', which depicts California, the 'absolute West', as '[a]n island of forgetting'[7] constantly in flight from the possibility of becoming a defined *polis* with a fixed *ethos*. Here LA expresses the inevitable tendency of 'untainted spaces to regress westward', evading mapping and containment: LA as 'capital of the world'

> because it isn't a European or East Coast-type city. It's not a city with an appearance of unity around some ecclesiastical, administrative, or economic center. It's a checkers game, along whose highways and 40-mile-long boulevards squares are marked off that can always only be temporarily occupied [...].[8]

The city whose 'language of design, architecture, and urbanism [...] is the language of movement'[9] is here addressed as the embodiment of a dynamic defined by the 'wanderings of the center', by chronic incompletion, and by a nebulous sprawl whose mapping is impossible:

> LA shows us rather what the ancient capitals lost, one after the other, in their wish, or their destiny, to be fixed permanently in one place: that a capital is not locatable, that it has no center, that in the heart of the Empire lies the belly of a white nomad, that the survey of L.A., an unsettled basin, always has to be done again and again.

'LA' names a peculiarly sustained embodiment of the general tendency: as Empire creeps east, potency (the 'belly' that the ministrations of the 'head' of administration and centralization chronically fail to conquer) spreads west, opening up a series of new 'capitals' or 'centers' each of which retrospectively designates its forerunners as part of its history. This self-externalization recalls the cunning fox fish described in Detienne and Vernant's book on *Cunning Intelligence in Greek Culture and Society*:

> There is [...] a fish which is reputed to be able to get itself out of an inextricable situation. As soon as it is caught on a hook it swims rapidly up and severs the line half way up or sometimes even higher. Plutarch tells us more about it: 'It generally avoids bait but if it is caught it gets rid of it. Thanks to its energy and flexibility' it is able to change its body and turn it inside out (*strephein*) so that the interior becomes the exterior: the hook falls out. Aelian provides full confirmation on the subject of this maneuver. 'It unfolds its internal organs and turns them inside out, divesting itself of its body as if it were a shirt. This fish turns itself inside out like a glove. It is the ultimate in reversal. And the name given this aquatic creature by the Greeks is 'fox fish'.[10]

Rather than bringing the dignity of the origin to the center of power, then, the European should come to pillage the nomadism of the center, the 'migratory movement' that is the real dynamism of the contemporary world...except that with every attempt to violate and seize this secret of power and youth, the city turns itself inside out and escapes. In words reminiscent of the delirious opening of *Libidinal Economy*, Lyotard affirms that the labyrinth 'isn't some complicated construction where you get lost—it's the body's capacity to undo its own apparent voluminousness, to devaginate itself'—and that LA is precisely such a sprawling labyrinthine body intractable to a synoptic view, a monster whose streets

> are organs expelled from a city in the process of turning itself inside out. The Western deserts are dotted with these weird limbs.[11]

The eversion of LA urbanism is, as Lyotard suggests,[12] relayed at scale by Californian modernist architecture with its 'interpenetration of indoor and outdoor spaces', which 'started with the useful advantage that the difference between indoors and outdoors was never as clearly defined there, nor as defensive, as it had been in Europe'.[13] According to the dominant theory, this mode of architecture 'us[es] the Californian opportunity to make a European dream come true';[14] following Lyotard's dualism between modern façade and postmodern interface, 'concepts of front and back dissolve because there are no façades to attach them to'.[15] The Fitzpatrick–Leland House, with its decentered complex of interlocking volumes evincing no dominant orientation or itinerary, could be seen as exemplary here, although we should note that Schindler's distinctive contribution lay far more in his attentive and inventive architectural responses to the specific requirements of local terrain and climate than in any straightforward transposition of modernism from Old to New World.

In short, the distinction what we might call the *synoptic* and *diauditory* models suggest that two different modes of urban organization and experience, reiterated in models of the 'apprenticeship in culture'[16] (the exhibition) correspond ultimately to the respective privileging of visual and auditory experience. This was seemingly the reasoning behind *Les Immatériaux*'s fragmentary organisation of space, and in particular its pioneering use of a radio headphone system. In explaining this, Lyotard refers back to his Californian experience and the 'nebula' of the LA conurbation:

This spatial layout which is in the process of taking shape will itself manifest, within the exhibition, many of the principles that I have described a little abstractly: firstly, the passage from one zone to another should be compared to the passage from one reception zone to another when a driver drives across a large metropolis. When you go from the Mexican border to Santa Barbara you have to retune the radio because you change transmitter; speech and music fade out and become noise, and you have to retune in order to find other speech, other music, you join them in mid-flow, and they are independent of each other. This nebulous aspect of which I spoke earlier, then, we hope to reproduce it through this device.[17]

The contingency, disorientation, and multiple overlapping zones of Lyotardian 'postmodern space-time'[18] would be attuned to the ear because they mark the rescinding of the modern dream of a spatial-visual synopsis allowing one to map out a project—for example, a city—as a logical, unified, and contained entity:

Descartes complains—or at least pretends to complain—that these cities were not constructed rationally but were made bit by bit [...] whereas if a city could be constructed, as we would say today, to plan—that is to say first of all on paper—then we would see clearly in this city, we would be able to orient ourselves in it very easily. The method being, at least in this text, in Descartes's eyes (at least this particular Descartes) something like a plan of domination specifying the procedures to be employed in order to master an object of knowledge.[19]

If the movement of resynthesis thematized in Hecker's intervention may be understood in terms of this dualism and its cognates, it is an operation that is no longer so strictly historicized. Hecker's operations move sequentially between synopsis and eversion. Texture synthesis begins with a movement from diauditory to synoptic, as the algorithm distils invariants from a sound texture. The resulting model is then deployed diachronically, extrapolating the characteristic features of the texture. The molecular analysis of natural odors yields a structural chemical model, whose manipulation and resynthesis reveals unforeseen connections between apparently discrete phenomenological scent-spaces. The movement is never without remainder—resynthesis is never simply a return to what was analyzed. The visitor completes the work, playing their own part in the production of difference along with the incidence of artefacts and byproducts. *Resynthesizers* introduces us into a multimodal space where this ongoing process of resynthesis plays out continually, in constant movement 'from the gaze [...] to the ear and an art of time'.[20] It will inevitably be experienced as '*unmasterable*';[21] to expect a string of words to make it any less so would be nonsense.

1 J.-F. Lyotard, 'After Six Months of Work... (1984)', tr. R. Mackay in Y. Hui and A. Broeckmann (eds.), *30 Years Les Immatériaux: Art, Science, Theory* (Lüneberg: Meson Press, 2015), 29–70: 45.

2 Lyotard, 'After Six Months...', 40. As 'proof' of the fact that contemporary or postmodern reading is listening, Lyotard observes 'that a natural voice or a synthetic voice could very well transmit this readable message were we not able to read it.' An observation that makes the necessary link between the use of screens in *Resynthesizers* and the use of synthetic voices in previous projects *FAVN* and *Inspection*.

3 Ibid. Note that one of the pioneering aspects of *Les Immatériaux* was Lyotard's invitation to a number of prominent thinkers to collaborate on an electronic text, published as *Épreuves d'écriture*.
4 J.-F. Lyotard, *Pacific Wall*, tr. B. Boone (Venice, CA: The Lapis Press, 1989).
5 Ibid., 29.
6 Ibid., 25–26.
7 Ibid., 27.
8 Ibid., 29.
9 R. Banham, *Los Angeles: The Architecture of Four Ecologies*, (Berkeley, CA: University of California Press, 2000), 5.
10 M. Detienne and J.-P. Vernant, *Cunning Intelligence in Greek Culture and Society* (Chicago: University of Chicago Press, 1991), 36–37.
11 Lyotard, *Pacific Wall*, 30–31.
12 Lyotard, 'After Six Months...', 57–58: 'to no longer conserve the opposition between inside and outside, but on the contrary, by means of lighting and transparency, to place the interior outside and the exterior inside'.
13 Banham, *Los Angeles*, 39.
14 Ibid., 171
15 Ibid.
16 Lyotard, 'After Six Months...', 47.
17 Ibid., 65.
18 Ibid., 53.
19 Ibid., 34.
20 Ibid., 52.
21 Ibid., 42.

LIBRETTI FOR RESYNTHESIZERS

ROBIN MACKAY

INFRA ESSENTIAL TOPOLOGY
ACCIDENTAL DISCLOSURE
RESIDUAL OLFACTIVE DEBRIS
TRUNCATED ARTEFACT
SYNTHETIC BYPRODUCT
MOLECULAR ASSEMBLY
DATA INFUSED MATERIAL
UNWHOLE PREPARATION
FOR ANTERIOR SENSORIUM
STRUCTURE LATCH TO RECEPTOR
PRIMAL COMFORT ANALOG
MILK AND HONEY
DELUXE ANTISEPTIC LEISURE
ELEMENTAL OVERDOSE
BRINE ABSTRACTED OZONE
SELECTIVE THALASSIC TREND
UNNATURAL CONFLUENCE
ON AND UNDER SKIN
ALCHEMICAL INTERFACE
RECESSIVE INTIMACY
ACCELERATED REGRESSION
CORPOREAL MEMORIES
UNLISTED COMMS CHANEL
MAMAS OF ANOTHER
NOW ADRIFT AND TRANSITING
CYBERNETIC RESORT
POOLSIDE SOUVENIR
2021 SANITISER DRYDOWN
AROMATIC NUCLEUS
ICE CREAM ON THE BEACH
VAST METALLIC TIDE
INCOMPLETE COMPOUND
AND THE NAME
GIVEN THIS AQUATIC CREATURE
NATAL VANILLOCEANIC ANOMALY
SMELL GOOD BABE
BIOSYNTHETIC MIME
THE FUGITIVE
ANONYMOUS AND IMMATERIAL
TRIGGER OF INTERNAL TRANSPORT

seq _1

CALIFORNIATED EUPHORIA
OF RETURNING HOME
TO THE GREAT OUTDOORS
A CITY EVERTED
UNASSIGNABLE PARTS
SPRAWL OF WEIRD LIMBS
VIVE LE ROI BATI
NO OLD WORLD DEBT
UNTAINTED SPACES
REGRESS WESTWARD
ENTRAILS EXTERNALISED
LIKE A GLOVE
HEAD DRIFTS OFF
COME TO LOSE YOUR CULTURE
NEBULA IN MOTION
URBAN CHESS GAME
ALL ABSORBING WHITE NOISE
SPACE MADE PLASTIC
MULTITIERED TRANSLUCENCY
FACADELESS CRYSTALLINE
VOLUMETRIC INTERLOCK
DISORIENTED ANTIPROMENADE
WRAPPED AROUND SPACE
OPEN AND DEFENCELESS
NO DOMINANT PATH
A DIAUDITORY WALK
NATURE INTERNALISED
SLOPE ADHERENT
LOCKED TO CLIMATE CONTROL
THE BUILDING, OR THIS ROOM
IS ALREADY A MESSAGE
EMPTY REAL ESTATE
UNLOCATABLE CAPITAL
UNTIL IT HITS THE WALL
STRESS FRACTURES IN TITANIUM
SPACE INFORMED
ADVANCED DOMESTIC MODEL
AREA FIELD ZONE
OF PERCEPTUAL RESONANCE
AS YET UNENCLOSED

seq _2

ABANDON SYNOPTIC AMBITION
WRITE WITH SLOGANS
LITERAL CAR CRASH READING
AN EYE THAT LISTENS
OR AN EAR THAT DRIVES
RETUNING MID FLOW
MULTIPLE RECEPTION ZONES
FREEWAY CLEAR
A NATURAL OR SYNTHETIC VOICE
COULD VERY WELL TRANSMIT
IMPOSSIBLE SYNOPSIS
THIS READABLE MESSAGE
OUR ENDLESS SCROLL
THESE BROKEN IMPRESSIONS
SUBSTRING COMPONENT
LANGUAGE THE RESISTOR
TINCTURE SIGNAL
THOUGHT WITHOUT IDENTITY
CULTIVATED GRAPHEME
IN CARVED GRAINS
TRANSFORMERS AT OUR DISPOSAL
QUESTIONS OF WHERE TO START
RETURN INTERMINABLY
SENSE TOO DEFINITE CANCELS
ESSENTIALLY, LISTENERS
A TEXT, IMPLIED
QUAVERING DOUBLE STATE
SUPREME CONDENSOR OF ALL
TRANSLATION PROBLEMS
BLIND BUT INDISPENSABLE
SYNTHESIS OF EXTERIORITIES
THIS READING IS
NOT PROPERLY SPEAKING
A VISION
SCREENED LISTENING
MY GLOSS BODIES FORTH
TRIALS OF WRITING
MACHINE TONGUE 1985
DESTABILISING MARKERS
ELECTROPHORETIC MIGRATIONS

seq _3

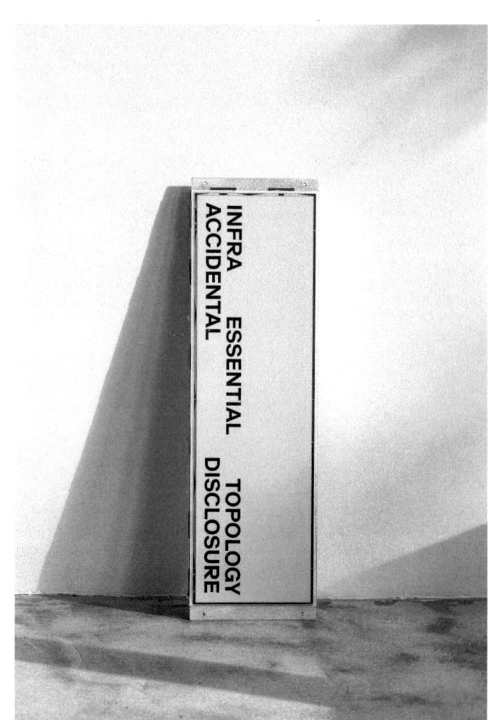

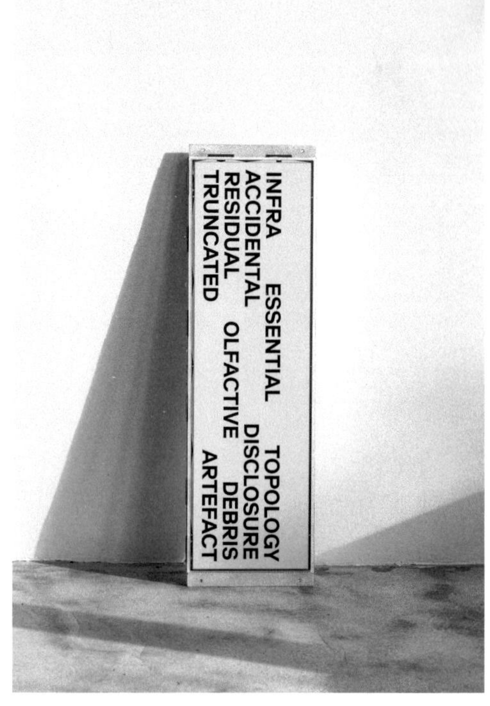

seq _1_01
seq _1_03

seq _1_02
seq _1_04

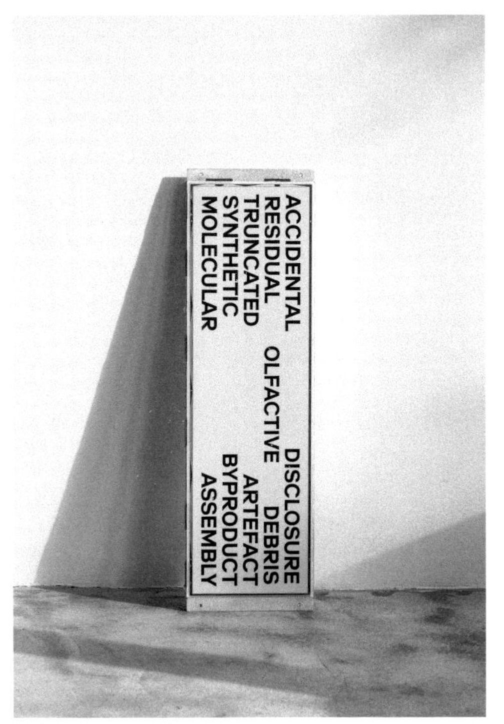

seq _1_05

seq _1_06

seq _1_07

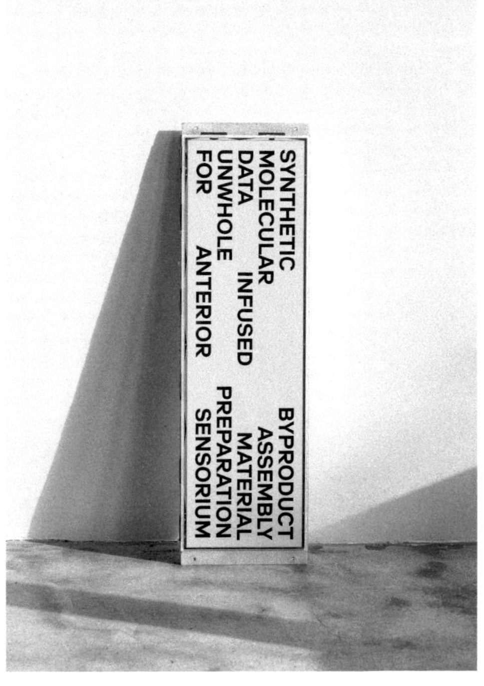

seq _1_08

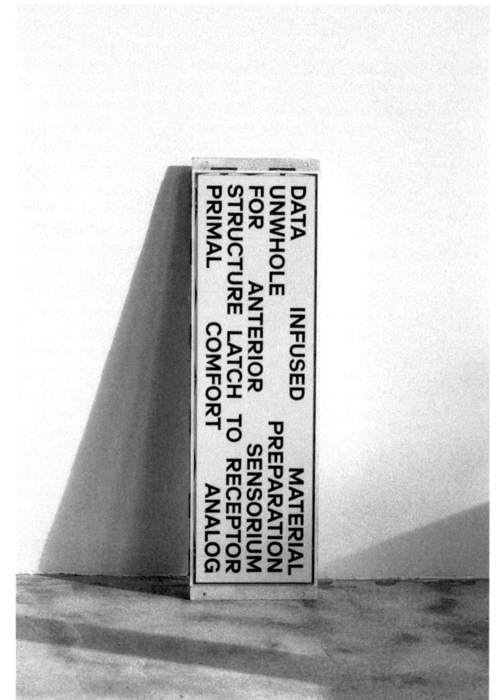

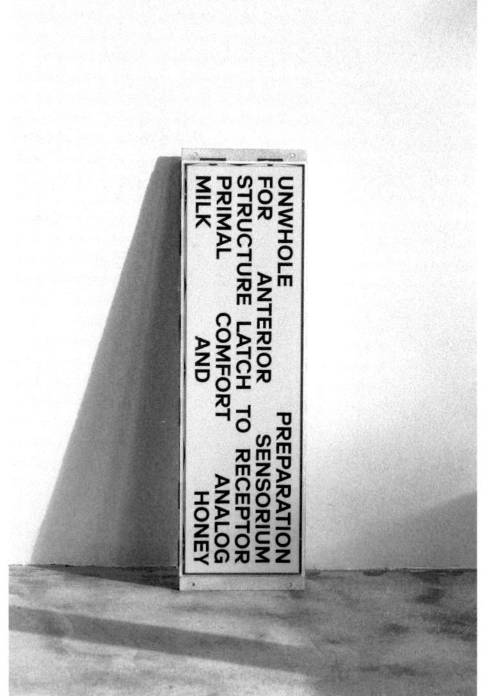

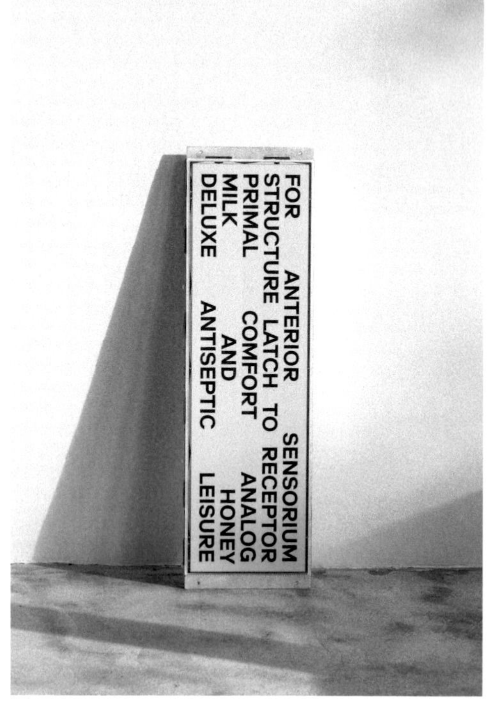

seq _1_09
seq _1_11

seq _1_10
seq _1_12

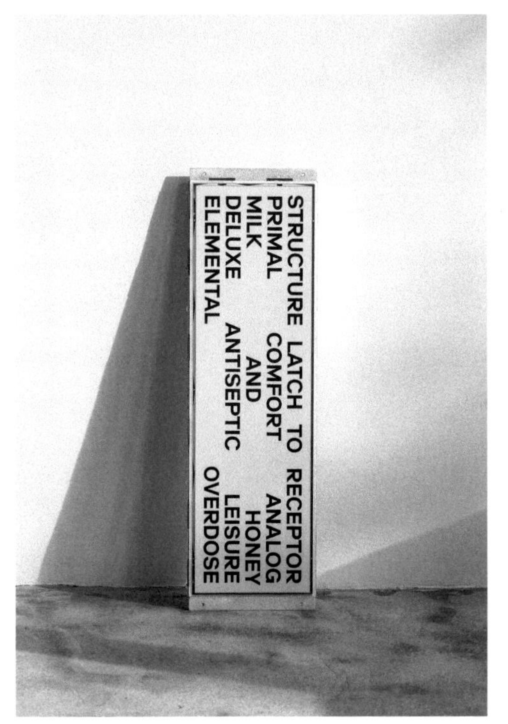

seq _1_13
seq _1_15

seq _1_14
seq _1_16

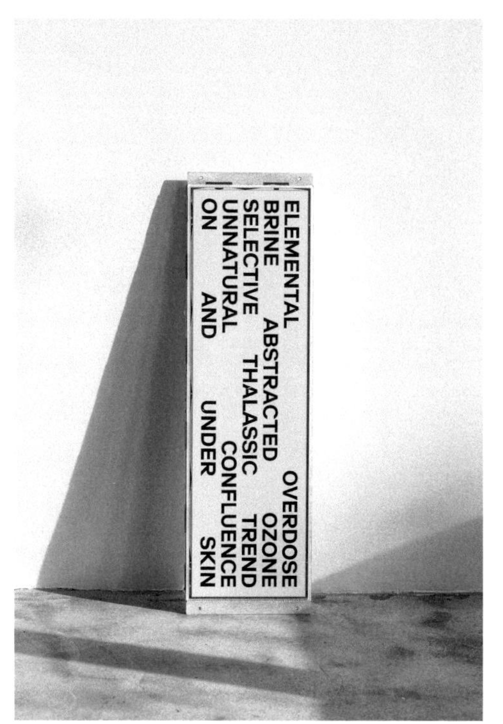

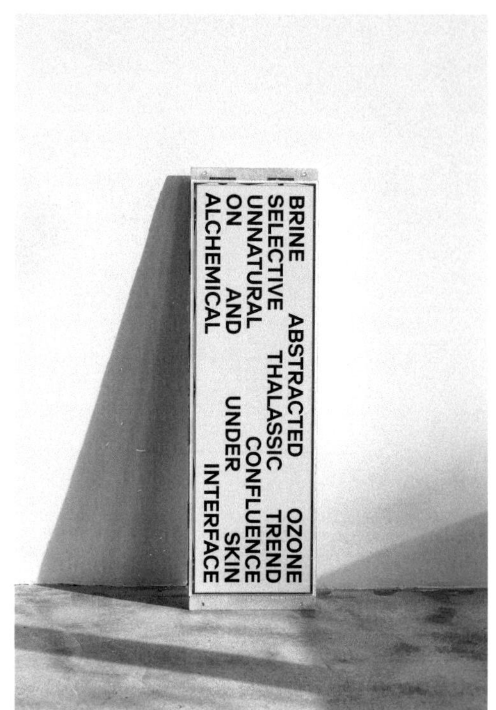

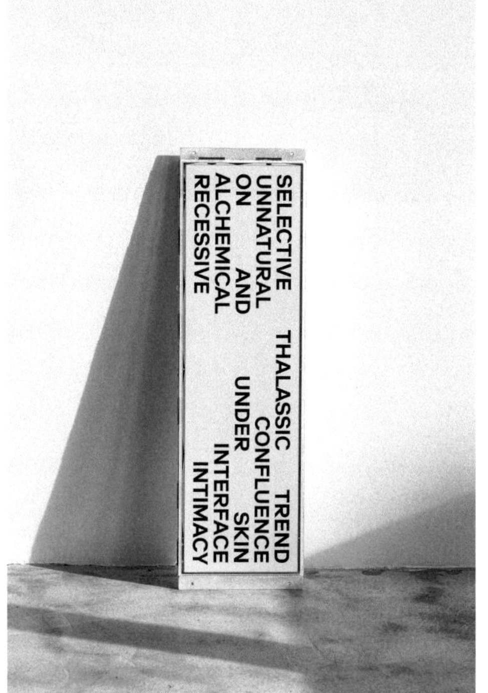

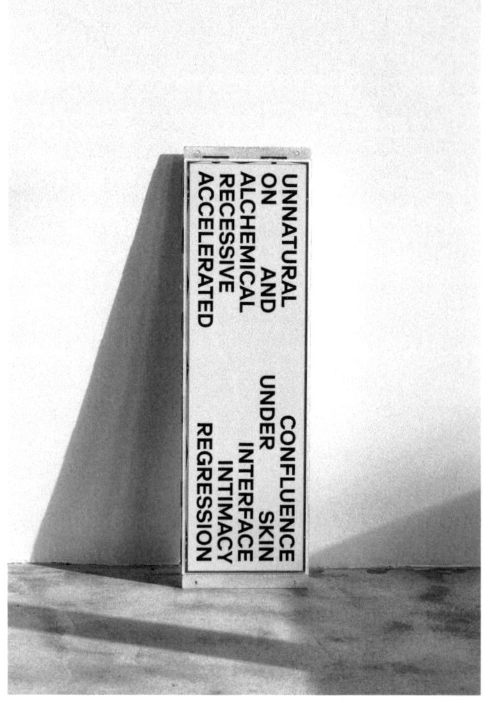

seq _1_17
seq _1_19

seq _1_18
seq _1_20

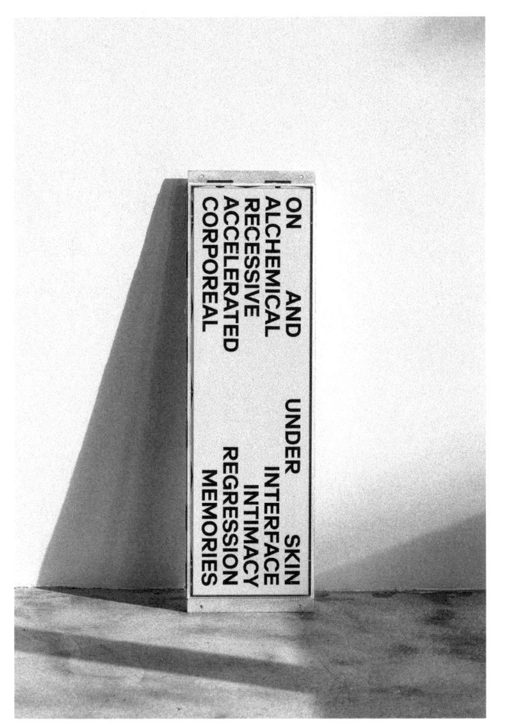

seq _1_21

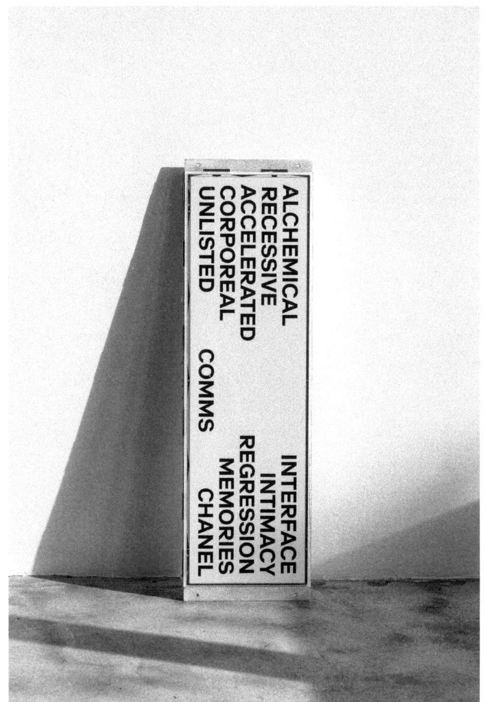

seq _1_22

seq _1_23

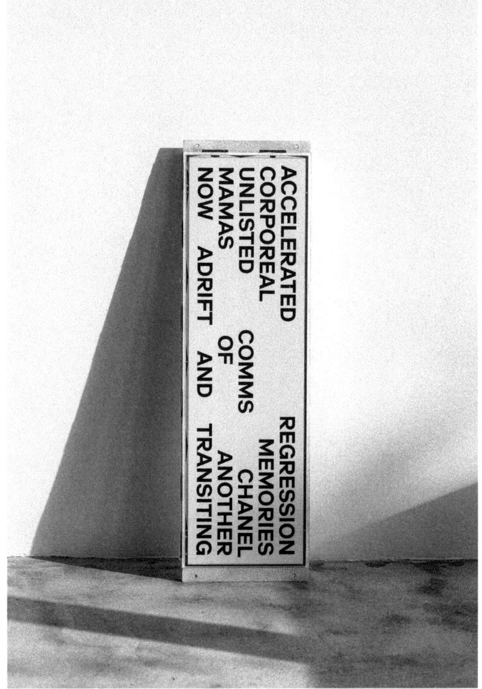

seq _1_24

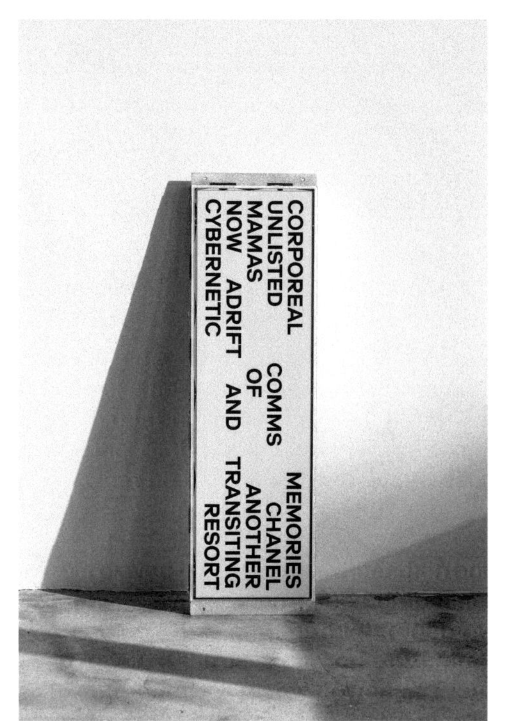

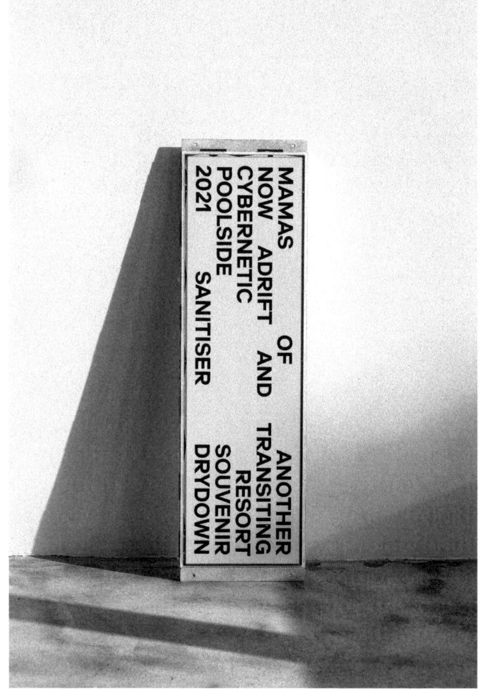

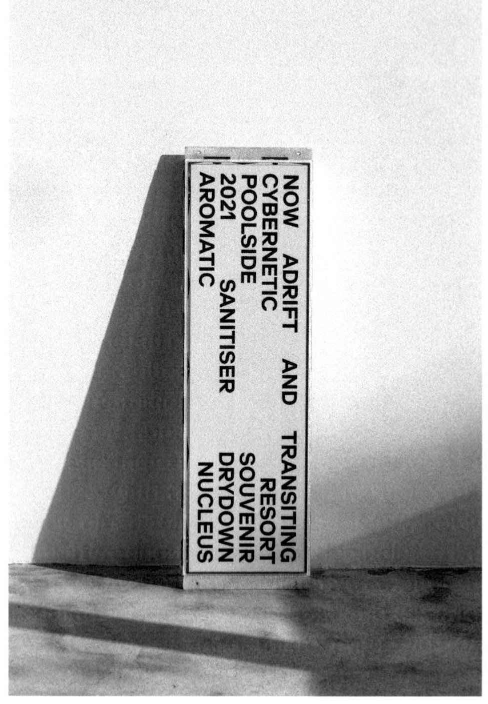

seq _1_25
seq _1_27

seq _1_26
seq _1_28

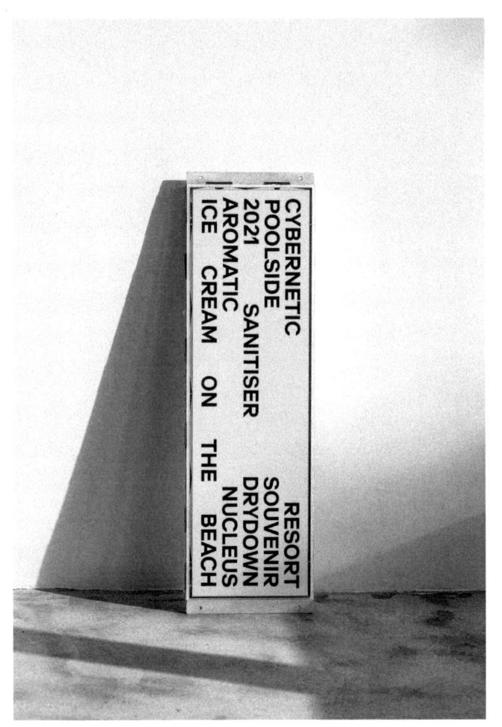

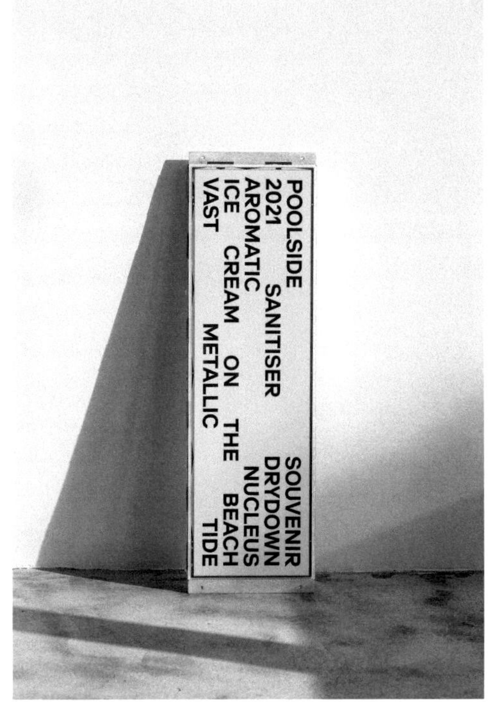

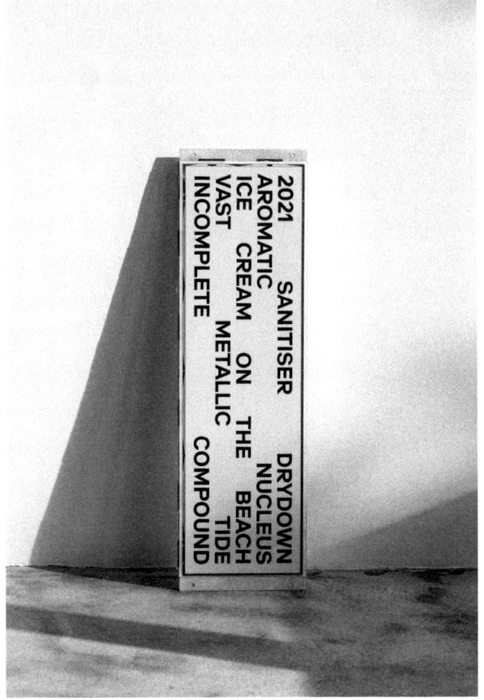

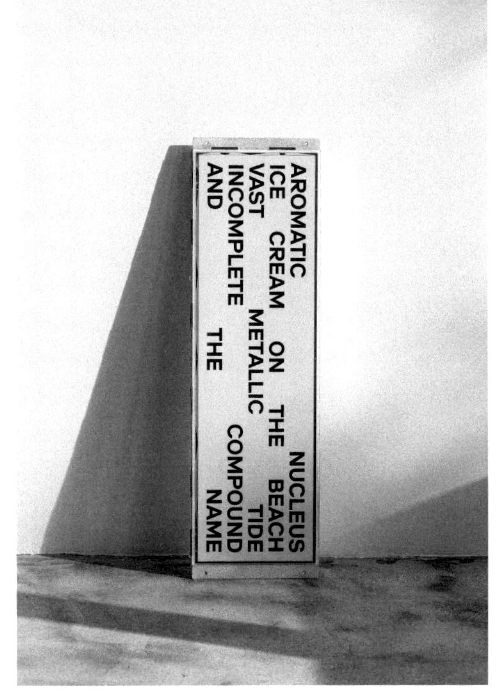

seq _1_29
seq _1_31

seq _1_30
seq _1_32

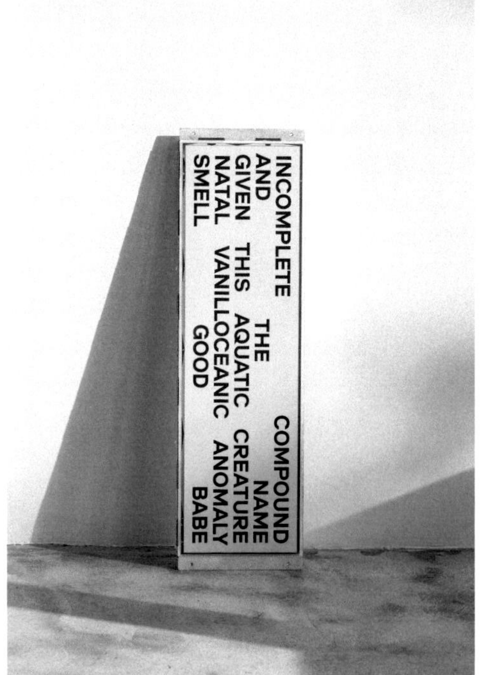

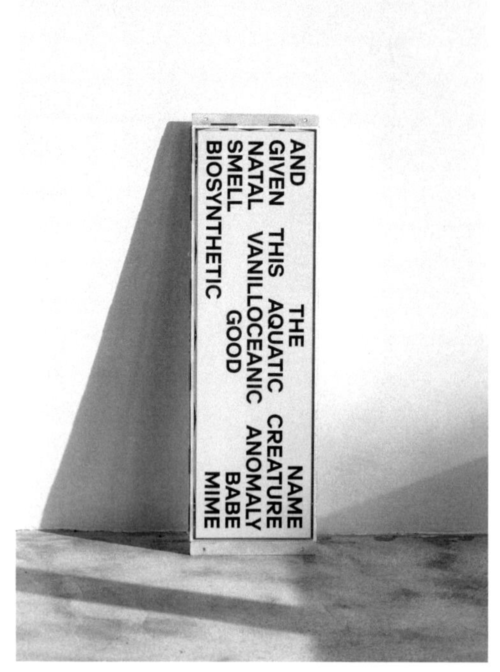

seq _1_33
seq _1_35

seq _1_34
seq _1_36

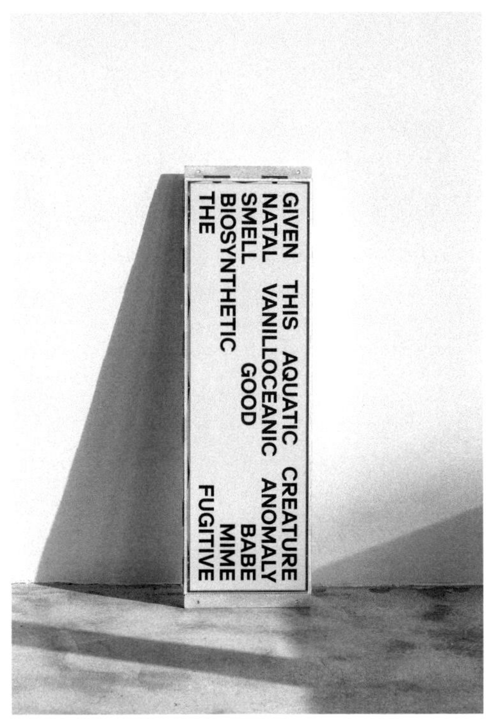

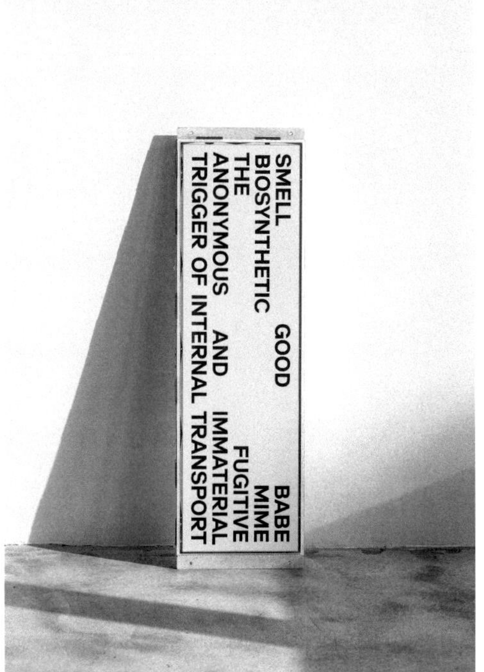

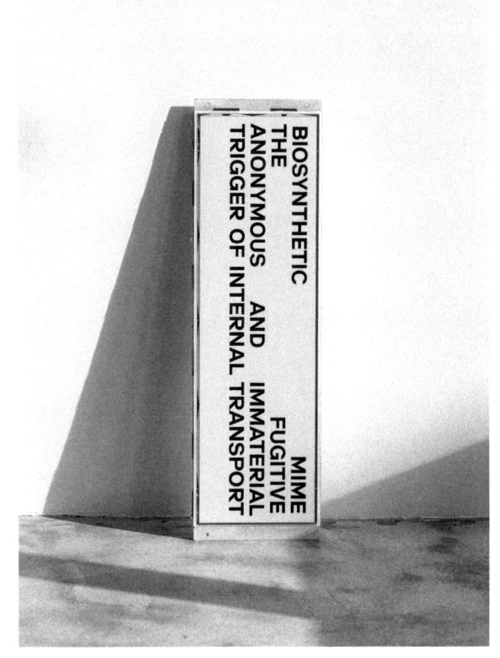

seq _1_37
seq _1_39

seq _1_38
seq _1_40

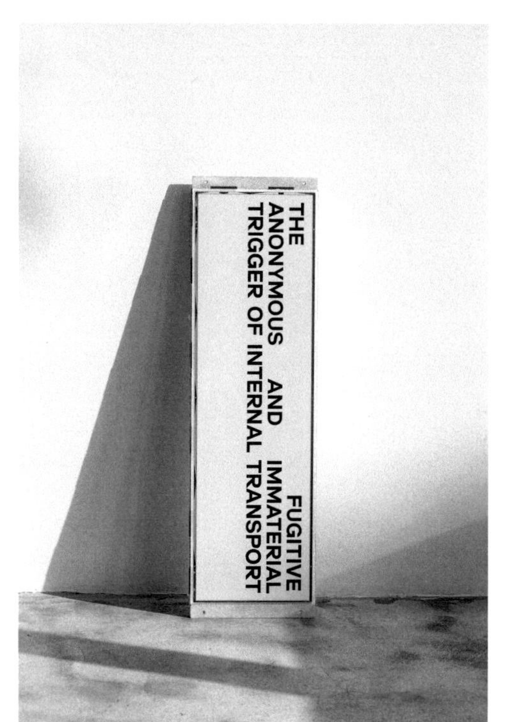

seq _1_41

seq _1_42

seq _1_43

ECHOING RESYNTHESIS

WENDY HUI KYONG CHUN AND ALEX H. BARNETT

From student papers written by chatbots to deepfake images produced by generative image engines, technologies designed to echo and reflect human creativity and reality seem poised instead to overwhelm and engulf them. In one week in March 2023 alone, tabloids and more reputable news sources featured stories about 'really scary' and fundamentally 'disruptive' fake images of Donald Trump's arrest and the Pope in Balenciaga.[1] The message seems plain: machine synthesis is killing truth, and we, like Narcissus, will languish in place, obsessed with images we mistake for reality.

Perhaps, but this presumes that this situation is new—and that there are two distinct types of machine (and indeed human) synthesis: slavish repetition that faithfully represents and presents itself, and masterful and imaginative acts that engender reality. Stories of early cinemagoers ducking in response to images of fast-moving trains and Marshall McLuhan's diagnosis of modern 'Western Man' as Narcissus—fascinated by media that extend and amputate human sense perception—reveal that this situation, however novel, is not unprecedented.[2] To unpack the complexities of synthesis, we turn here to the work of Florian Hecker. We begin with mathematical and critical explanations of Hecker's use of resynthesis in *FAVN* and *Resynthese FAVN,* then move to draw out the Echo/echoes that haunt these projects, so as to shift the focus away from self-knowledge and master-slave relations toward repetitive yet ethical embraces.

Analysis — Synthesis

As noted by Robin Mackay, Michael Newman, and Ina Blom among others, Florian Hecker's work brilliantly enacts resynthesis—the synthetic recreation of what has been previously synthesized—to create an 'intramachinic atmosphere [...] machinic milieus and realities that stretch what it means to be sensed and sense'.[3] *Resynthese FAVN*, which debuted in 2017 at Kunsthalle Wien and played at REDCAT while Hecker's Equitable Vitrines *Resynthesizers* exhibition was live at the Fitzpatrick-Leland House, epitomizes this practice. Most obviously, *Resynthese FAVN*, developed with Axel Röbel at IRCAM, technically resynthesizes Hecker's 2016 *FAVN*, which debuted in 2016 at Frankfurt's Alte Oper. This resynthesis, however, is itself recursive, for Hecker produced *FAVN* via technical resynthesis—making it the latest outcome of a process that breaks down the very opposition between synthesis and analysis. *FAVN* was created in two stages: firstly, by generating '47 blocks of sound of duration equal to 21 seconds, and spatialized across three audio channels', synthesized by essentially mid-twentieth-century technology—'the tools of the electroacoustic studio, such as oscillators and modulators'—and then subsequently via a 'resynthesis' of these sounds using distinctly twenty-first-century tools of signal processing and machine learning.[4] This second resynthesis stage is at the heart of *FAVN*, and of many of Hecker's more recent pieces; to make clear how and why this matters, below we offer an accessible sketch of how it works.[5]

First, the signal is analyzed. The mathematical representation of recorded sound pressure—a one-dimensional (1D) function x(*t*)—is broken down into its 1D 'wavelet components', that is, the set of pure tone frequencies l present at each time *t*. Recall that the audible frequency range is from around 20 to 20,000 Hz (cycles per second). The resulting 2D 'image' is called the spectrogram S_1x [see Fig. 1], and is similar to a musical staff notation for the sound, or to the set of holes in a player piano roll scrolling from the right. Interestingly, the *phase* (precise alignment) of the wavelet components is discarded, leaving only their *magnitude*. This time-frequency magnitude representation resembles how our ears communicate signals to our auditory cortex. Secondly, building on this, the so-called *joint time-frequency scattering transform* S_2x applies another level of analysis:[6] it breaks the 2D spectrogram image S_1x into its 2D wavelet components, much as the early retinal layers in the eye extract edge features with different scales and orientations. The resulting object S_2x is actually a *4D function*—and therefore very hard to visualize—that captures the magnitude of the signal at time *t*, frequency l, pulsation rate a, and modulation scale b [see bottom of Fig. 1]. This is similar to the first layer of neural processing found experimentally in the auditory cortex of animals.[7] Such analysis is computationally quick because of the invention of the *fast Fourier transform* (FFT).[8]

In *FAVN*, the analyzed signals x(*t*) are the 47 electroacoustic blocks of sound. The resynthesis stage uses a computational algorithm to adjust a new white noise (hiss) signal—call it y(*t*)—towards having the same time-frequency scattering transform S_2y as one of the analyzed S_2x. This adjustment is made computationally by a gradient-descent iteration—a simple optimization technique using 'backpropagation'—which successively improves the match. In *FAVN*, fifty such iterations are auralized in sequence, exposing to the listener the algorithm's slow deformation of the white noise into something that our perceptual systems find similar in timbre and style to x.

These scattering transform methods came from mathematical signal processing research groups, including that of Stéphane Mallat, who is interested in realistic audio and visual texture synthesis, classification, source separation, style transfer, and many other machine learning 'challenges'.[9] *FAVN* may be interpreted as style transfer from a given audio source onto white noise—that is, a form of texture synthesis. More broadly, over the last decade, stochastic gradient descent (SGD) applied to the parameters of deep convolutional neural networks (similar to the wavelets above) has revolutionized machine learning, allowing the generation of high-quality 'deepfake' imitations of human artistic creativity (e.g., DALL-E).[10] The question of just why SGD on deep networks works so well is now an incredibly active worldwide research topic in the mathematics of high-dimensional function representation, and the wavelet-based work of Mallat and others is one of the very few promising approaches to answering it.[11]

In *Resynthese FAVN*, developed later with Axel Röbel at IRCAM, Hecker adds a third stage to the process: *FAVN* itself is resynthesized again from a signal that combines the so-called original *FAVN* with seeded noise (derived from an adaptation of a Xenakis piece), via eight different versions that converge over time.[12] Here the new idea is to consider the cross-correlation (CC) between perceptual frequency bands (i.e., different 'horizontal slices' of the spectrogram). The noise seed is then iteratively adjusted to bring its CC into closer alignment with that of the desired signal—the original *FAVN* piece. These CC coefficients are quite similar to the 'moments' (and higher-order moments) that are matched to perform audio and visual texture synthesis by Mallat and colleagues, thus connecting Hecker's work to the cutting edge of machine learning research.

As this technical description makes clear, Hecker's work uses resynthesis—the process of re-creating the artificial—to bring together the usually opposed movements of analysis—the breaking down of phenomenon into simpler constituents or logically proceeding from effects to causes[13]—and synthesis—the production of an organic compound from simpler elements or the movement from causes to effects.[14] Crucially, as Mackay has stressed, this resynthesis is never exact.[15] Just as a perfume's odor depends on who and what is present, the resynthesized sounds depend on environmental noise and the echo function of a room. If, as Gilles Deleuze once remarked, in a world defined by change, repetition 'is due to miracle rather than to law',[16] Hecker's works investigate what—machinically, perceptually—makes this miracle both possible and impossible. Because of this, according to Newman and Mackay, Hecker's resynthesis exposes us to radical doubt regarding our perceptions: 'we must ourselves "integrate" and "perpetuate" a work that offers no definitive conclusion, but instead activates contingencies of our sensory organs and exacerbates perceptual equivocation.'[17]

This radical doubt supplies the link between *FAVN's* technical and putatively thematic resyntheses. *FAVN* itself draws inspiration from Mallarmé's poem 'L'après-midi d'un Faune' (*The Afternoon of a Faun*) and Debussy's symphonic response to it, *Prélude à l'après-midi d'un Faune* (*Prelude to the Afternoon of a Faun*). Mallarmé's poem, often considered the greatest poem written in the French language owing to its play with the language, relays a faun's experience—or not—with two nymphs: one who apparently rejects him, and another who '*contraste comme brise du jour chaude dans ta toison* [compares to a hot wind through the fleece that blows at noon]'.[18] Waking from what seems like a dream, he tries to reconstruct his experiences with them, and the poem plays with the ambiguity of memory and origins, and the desire to perpetuate the sources of sexual desire, the effects of which are still felt on the senses and the body. Debussy's symphonic poem takes up these issues through timbre—that seemingly non-symbolizable difference between two sounds of the same pitch and amplitude (for example, a note played on a clarinet versus one played on a flute). As Mallarmé said of Debussy's *Prelude*, '*elle va encore plus loin, vraiment dans la nostalgie et la lumière, avec finesse, avec malaise, avec richesse* [it goes even further, really in nostalgia and light, with finesse, with discomfort, with richness]'.[19] Hecker's *FAVN* evokes issues surrounding late nineteenth-century psychophysics as well as Debussy's *Prélude*, but does so at a time when, as Newman stresses, timbre has become measurable.[20] The analysis-synthesis pairing, however, still invokes these issues, for, according to Mackay, it 'takes place not so much on the stage of the Alte Oper (which indeed is all but empty and hosts no "action") as in the intimacy of what Mallarmé called the "inner stage", where ambiguity and absence serve to evoke, between the lines, in the mind of the audience, an Idea that evades explicit presentation.'[21]

Yes, but for this to happen, we must identify with the protagonist, the faun. But do we have to be the *FAVN*, and upon whose inner stage does this drama play?

FAVN ←---→ Echo

Intriguingly, the scattering transform (S_2x described above) was inspired by the neurophysiological models devised by Shibab A. Shamma's group in which 'sound is decomposed by the cochlea into a wavelet transform, which is then convolved by a two-dimensional Gabor filter in the auditory cortex'.[22] This would seem to be a textbook case of how understanding biological specificities improves computational methods. However, this model not only erases bodily agency (since we also make sound in our ears);[23] it also introduces an animal interloper into the story, for the neurophysiological inner stage belongs to a ferret. For their model, Shamma's group did not experiment with humans but rather with ferrets. Ferrets have become human auditory model organisms because they hear what we hear (or are trained to a close approximation), and they can be sacrificed in the name of science: opened up, drugged, and fed intravenously, so that they do not pass out while hooked up to equipment to measure and map their cortical signals.[24] If we are the faun, then we are, as Stefan Helmreich has pointed out, chimerical: a combination of human and animal.[25]

Echoes haunt *FAVN* at both technical and thematic levels. An echo is a transformation (resynthesis) that replaces every feature of a signal with the so-called 'impulse response' of the acoustic space or room [see Fig. 2] to that signal. Mathematically this is called a *convolution*.[26] In practice, it is easy for a human to hear this impulse response—simply clap (an impulse) and listen. However, the effect depends on the listener's location and also, because humans absorb sound, the locations of other listeners. Echoes make every resynthesis different. Because of the mathematics of Fourier analysis, an echo may equally be described by a coloration (filtering) of the frequency content of a signal [see the lower part of Fig. 2]. A classic example of this is the conversion of white noise from our vocal cords into intelligible vowel sounds (colored noise) when we whisper. Mathematically speaking, this is simply the echo of various shapes of the vocal cavity: our mouths are small chambers of variable shape. Echo/filtering is thus a form of style transfer from the space/cavity onto the source signal.

At a thematic level, the story of Echo also colors and complicates the story of the faun—like Debussy's symphonic poem, it '*va encore plus loin*', albeit very differently. The stories of Echo are tragic, and her experiences with Pan, the uber-faun and god of nature, reveal the violence behind scattering waveforms, analyses, and unrequited desire. In Longus's *Daphnis and Chloe*, Echo is a virtuous and beautiful nymph who raised Pan's ire, because he 'envied her gift for music, and partly because he had failed to enjoy her beauty'.[27] He then 'inspired with frenzy the shepherds and the goatherds, who, like dogs or wolves, tore the maiden to pieces, and flung her limbs here and there, still quivering with song'. Thankfully, Earth, 'out of respect for the Nymphs, received and hid them in her bosom, where they still preserve their gift of song, and by the will of the Muses, speak and imitate all sounds, as the maiden did when alive'.

Echo's fragments then repeat 'the voices of men and Gods, musical instruments, and the cries of wild beasts', and even the music of Pan.

There is a less violent, if no less tragic, intertwining of Echo and man, one that, as Gayatri Spivak has argued, moves us away from analytic self-knowledge towards ethics as relation.[28] This Echo is about response and relation—the convolution of room and signal—and interruption and deferred embrace. It comes to us from Ovid's *Metamorphoses*,[29] in which Echo is a talkative nymph whom Jupiter commands to distract Juno while he dallies with other nymphs. Once this ruse is revealed, Juno punishes Echo by taking away her ability to form her own speech: Echo becomes an echo, condemned to repeat the words of others. One day while hiding in the woods, Echo falls in love with Narcissus and, seeing him, wants him to know of her passion but cannot tell him. But then, inadvertently, he helps her. He calls out, 'Is anyone here?', and she replies, 'Here'. Narcissus then looks everywhere and shouts, 'Come to me!' which she repeats. Seeing no one, he asks, 'Why do you run from me?' and then says, 'Here, let us meet together.' Echo replies 'Together', and then runs out of the woods to put her arms around his neck, in longing. He runs from her and cries, 'Away with these encircling hands! May I die before what's mine is yours.' She answers only, '*What's mine is yours!*'[30] Echo leaves broken-hearted, and she wastes away, her body becoming stone so that all that remains is her voice. And it is as a voice that she witnesses Narcissus's downfall—the moment in which he comes to know himself, for Narcissus is eventually punished for his cruelty not to Echo, but to another shunned would-be lover. He comes to a pond and falls in love with his image. In Ovid's tale, Echo repeats his dying words, 'Alas! Goodbye!'[31] and this is the Narcissus—primitive man child, fixated on his self-image and incapable of social relations—that we know thanks to Freud, Lacan, McLuhan, and many others.[32]

This Narcissus we have come to know, Spivak stresses, erases Echo, who nonetheless seeks to break through the text. And Spivak argues that critical theory—when it ignores Echo—locks itself into a destructive and unethical 'self-knowledge', missing how the Narcissus-Echo pair reveal 'a punishment that is finally a dubious reward quite outside the borders of the self [...]. Echo in Ovid is staged as the instrument of possibility of a truth not dependent upon intention, a reward uncoupled from, and indeed set free from, the recipient.'[33] In her deconstructive embrace, which seeks to disrupt self-knowledge (the 'fly from me' that Ovid glosses over), Echo instantiates ethics and relation. Ethics, Spivak stresses, 'are not a problem of knowledge but a call to a relationship'.[34] The call and problem are 'in a deconstructive embrace: Narcissus and Echo. If we see ourselves only as subjects (or "selves") of a knowledge that cannot relate and see the "self" as writing, our unavoidable ethical decisions will be caught in the more empirical, less philosophical "night of non-knowledge," [...]. If we move to Echo as the (un)intending subject of ethics, we are allowed to understand the mysterious responsibility of ethics, that its subject cannot comprehend.'[35]

To return to Hecker's work and to our first examples, unintended echoes disrupt the cycle of analysis and synthesis, ensuring that the paths from cause to effect and back again are never identical. Perhaps the miracle is not that things repeat, but that they do not. To move away from the darkness of self-knowledge—the obsession with generated images and texts that seem to mirror human creativity—we need to embrace the materials and echoes that have always colored our world in inhuman ways. To do so, we need to remain with the gap between synthesis and analysis—and to dwell with the repetition that, nonetheless, always flies from us.

1 I. Stanley-Becker and N. Nix, 'Deepfake Trump Arrest Photos Show Disruptive Power of AI,' *The Washington Post*, March 22, 2023, <https://www.washingtonpost.com/politics/2023/03/22/trump-arrest-deepfakes/>; Erin Keller, 'Pope Francis in Balenciaga Deepfake Fools Millions: "Definitely Scary"' *New York Post*, March 27, 2023, <https://nypost.com/2023/03/27/pope-francis-in-balenciaga-deepfake-fools-millions-definitely-scary/>.

2 T. Gunning, 'An Aesthetic of Astonishment: Early Film and the (in)Credulous Spectator', in *Film Theory: Critical Concepts in Media and Cultural Studies*, eds. Philip Simpson, Andrew Utterson, and K. J. Shepherdson (London: Routledge, 2004); Marshall McLuhan, *Understanding Media: The Extensions of Man* (Cambridge, MA: MIT Press, 1994).

3 R. Mackay, 'FAVN', *readthis.wtf*, 2016, <http://readthis.wtf/writing/favn/>; M. Newman, 'Sensation and the Measure of Timbre: Florian Hecker's *Resynthese FAVN* Revisiting Mallarmé's Scene', in F. Hecker, *Halluzination, Perspektive, Synthese*, ed. V. Müller (Berlin and Vienna: Sternberg Press/Kunsthalle Wien, 2019); I. Blom, 'Intramachinic Atmospheres: Florian Hecker and the Fabrication of Sensing', 2021, <https://www.goethe.de/ins/us/en/sta/los/ver.cfm?event_id=22473894>; Ina Blom, 'Sound Effects: Ina Blom on the Art of Florian Hecker', *Artforum*, April 2021, <https://www.artforum.com/print/202104/ina-blom-on-the-art-of-florian-hecker-85251>.

4 V. Lostanlen and F. Hecker, 'The Shape of RemiXXXes to Come: Audio Texture Synthesis with Time-Frequency Scattering' (arXiv, June 29, 2019), http://arxiv.org/abs/1906.09334, 3.

5 This complements the mathematical presentations of Lostanlen and Hecker, 'The Shape of RemiXXXes to Come' and J. Andén, V. Lostanlen, and S. Mallat, 'Joint Time-Frequency Scattering for Audio Classification', *2015 IEEE 25th International Workshop on Machine Learning for Signal Processing (MLSP)*, <https://doi.org/10.1109/MLSP.2015.7324385>, 1–6.

6 Andén, Lostanlen, and Mallat, 'Joint Time-Frequency Scattering for Audio Classification'.

7 S.A. Shamma et al., 'Organization of Response Areas in Ferret Primary Auditory Cortex', *Journal of Neurophysiology* 69:2 (February 1, 1993): 367–83, <https://doi.org/10.1152/jn.1993.69.2.367>; T. Chi, P. Ru, and S.A. Shamma, 'Multiresolution Spectrotemporal Analysis of Complex Sounds', *The Journal of the Acoustical Society of America* 118:2 (August 2005): 887–906, <https://doi.org/10.1121/1.1945807>.

8 The reader may explore scattering transforms using the Kymatio software: M. Andreux et al., 'Kymatio: Scattering Transforms in Python', *Journal of Machine Learning Research* 21 (2020), <https://jmlr.org/papers/v21/19-047.html>.

9 S. Mallat, 'Understanding Deep Convolutional Networks', *Philosophical Transactions of the Royal Society A: Mathematical, Physical and Engineering Sciences* 374:2065 (April 13, 2016), <https://doi.org/10.1098/rsta.2015.0203>.

10 'DALL-E 2', <https://openai.com/product/dall-e-2>.

11 Mallat, 'Understanding Deep Convolutional Networks'."

12 A. Röbel, 'Sound Processing for the Production of *Resynthese FAVN*', in Hecker, *Halluzination, Perspektive, Synthese*. Regarding Iannis Xenakis' GENDYN and the concepts of Dynamic Stochastic Synthesis, see: Peter Hoffmann, "Music Out of Nothing? A Rigorous Approach to Algorithmic Com- position by Iannis Xenakis," PhD thesis, Technische Universität Berlin (2009).

13 'Analysis', *Oxford English Dictionary Online*, <https://www.oed.com/view/Entry/7046>.

14 'Synthesis', *Oxford English Dictionary Online*, <https://www.oed.com/view/Entry/196574>.

15 R. Mackay, 'Skin Games: A Primer', *readthis.wtf*, 2013, <http://readthis.wtf/writing/skin-games-a-primer/> .

16 G. Deleuze, *Difference and Repetition*, tr. P. Patton (New York: Columbia University Press, 1994), 2.

17 R. Mackay, 'Return of the Faun', in F. Hecker, *Formulations*, ed. S. Gaensheimer, M. Wandschneider and R. Mackay (London: Koenig Books, 2016), <http://readthis.wtf/writing/return-of-the-faun-formulations/>.

18 S. Mallarmé, *Collected Poems of Mallarmé: A Bilingual Edition*, tr. H.H. Weinfield (Berkeley, CA: University of California Press, 1994).

19 G. Pressnitzer, 'Claude Debussy: Prélude à l'après-midi d'un faune', *Esprits Nomades*, <https://www.espritsnomades.net/musiques/claude-debussy-prelude-a-lapres-midi-dun-faune/>.

20 Lostanlen and Hecker, 'The Shape of RemiXXXes to Come'; Newman, 'Sensation and the Measure of Timbre'.

21 Mackay, 'Return of the Faun'.

22 Andén, Lostanlen, and Mallat, 'Joint Time-Frequency Scattering for Audio Classification', 2.

23 R Probst, B L Lonsbury-Martin, and G K Martin, 'A Review of Otoacoustic Emissions', *J Acoust. Soc. Am.* 89:5 (May 1991): 2027–67. DOI: 10.1121/1.400897

24 Shamma et al., 'Organization of Response Areas in Ferret Primary Auditory Cortex'.

25 S. Helmreich, *Sounding the Limits of Life: Essays in the Anthropology of Biology and Beyond* (Princeton, NJ: Princeton University Press, 2015).

26 A.H. Barnett, ‘Convolution: Son et Lumière’, *Convolution. A Journal for Experimental Criticism* 1 (2009), <http://convolutionjournal.com/no-1>, available at <https://users.flatironinstitute.org/~ahb/papers/c.pdf>.

27 Longus, *Daphnis & Chloe*, tr. P. Turner (London: Penguin Classics, 1989), 84.

28 G.C. Spivak, ‘Echo’, *New Literary History* 24:1 (1993): 17–43, <https://doi.org/10.2307/469267>.

29 Ovid, ‘Metamorphoses’, tr. A.S. Kline, <https://ovid.lib.virginia.edu/trans/Ovhome.htm#askline>.

30 Ibid.

31 Ibid.

32 For more on this, see Spivak's ‘Echo’, and Wendy Hui Kyong Chun, ‘After McLuhan’ in *Re-Understanding Media: Feminist Extensions of Marshall McLuhan* (Durham, NC: Duke University Press, 2022), 225–232.

33 Spivak, ‘Echo’, 23–4.

34 Ibid., 32.

35 Ibid.

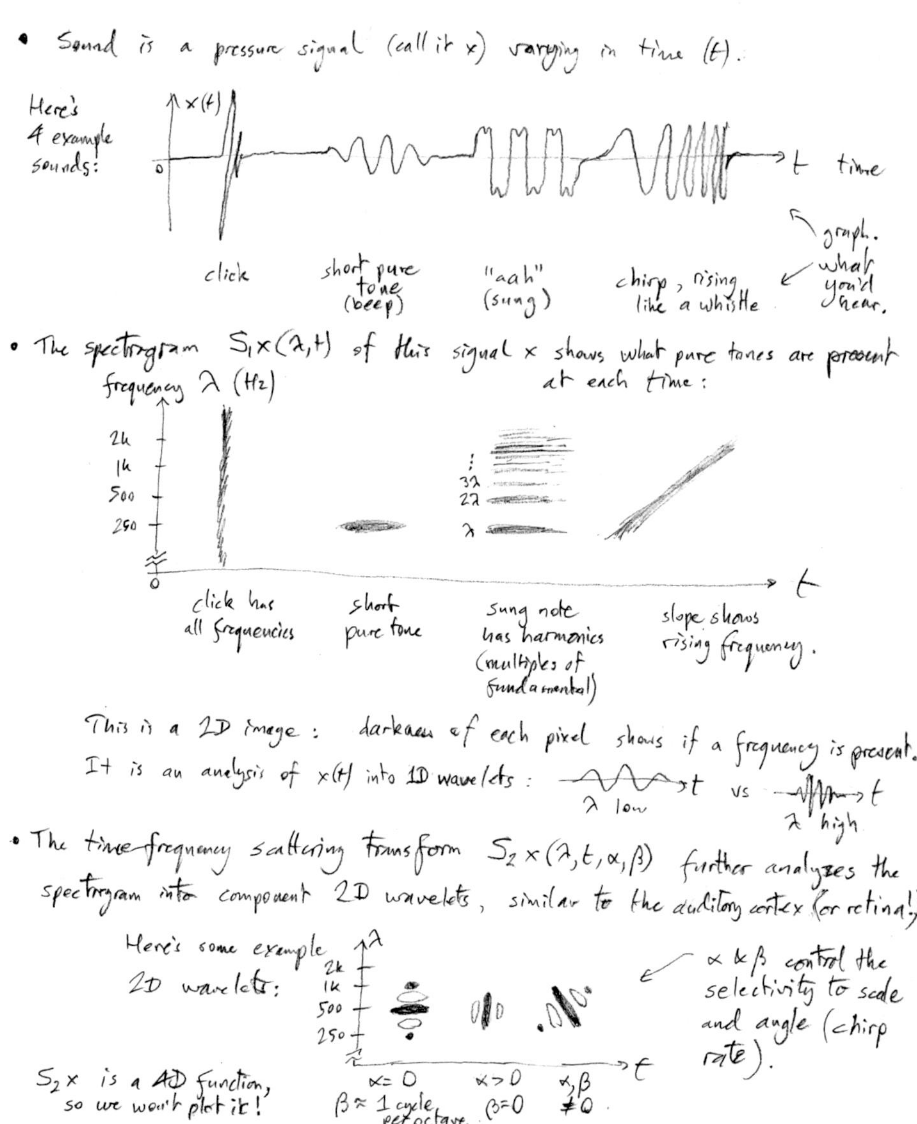
INSERT 1.
• Sound is a pressure signal (call it x) varying in time (t).
Here's 4 example sounds:
x(t)
0
t time
← graph. what you'd hear.
click
short pure tone (beep)
"aah" (sung)
chirp, rising like a whistle
• The spectrogram S₁x(λ,t) of this signal x shows what pure tones are present at each time:
frequency λ (Hz)
2k
1k
500
250
0
3λ
2λ
λ
t
click has all frequencies
short pure tone
sung note has harmonics (multiples of fundamental)
slope shows rising frequency.
This is a 2D image: darkness of each pixel shows if a frequency is present.
It is an analysis of x(t) into 1D wavelets: t vs t
λ low
λ high
• The time-frequency scattering transform S₂x(λ,t,α,β) further analyzes the spectrogram into component 2D wavelets, similar to the auditory cortex (or retina!)
Here's some example 2D wavelets:
λ
2k
1k
500
250
t
α = 0 β ≈ 1 cycle per octave
α > 0 β = 0
α, β ≠ 0
α & β control the selectivity to scale and angle (chirp rate).
S₂x is a 4D function, so we won't plot it!
• FAVN iteratively adjusts a noise signal until its S₂ matches that of a given sound.

Fig. 1

- An echo (the interaction of a signal with an acoustic space) can be viewed either 1) as a <u>convolution</u> with the impulse response function of the space/room:

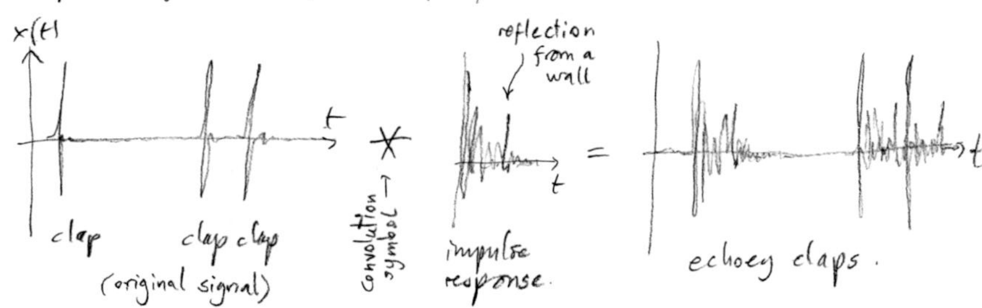

or 2) as a "coloration" (a basic style transfer, or spectral filtering) of the frequency content. This happens, for example, when one whispers different vowel sounds: the vocal track (an echoing space) colors via its formants the noise from the vocal cords:

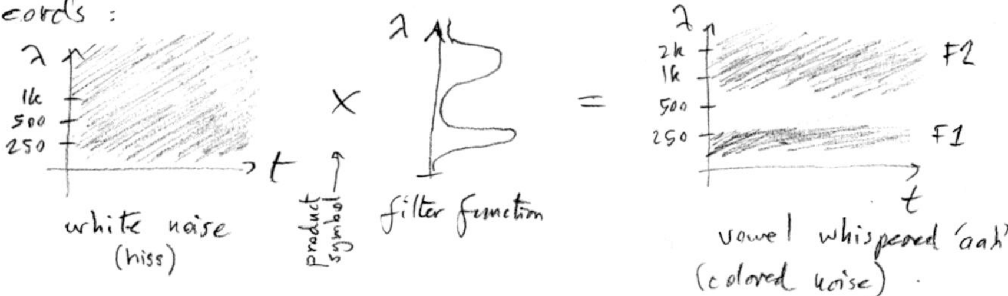

- The above two are mathematically equivalent, but:
  View 1) is useful for long echoes (> 50 ms, say), while view 2) for short echoes (very small spaces, cavities, vocal tracts...)

NEGATIVE INSTRUMENTALITY AND SYNTHETIC ABSTRACTION IN FLORIAN HECKER'S RESYNTHESIZERS

LUCIANA PARISI

To enter Florian Hecker's *Resynthesizers* is to be positioned at the end of aesthetics, or even routed toward a non-aesthetics: noise-information patterns instigate the artificial generation of sonic and olfactory axiomatics which place in tension the cognitive registering of audio-fragrant discreteness. This is the path via which art can be said to expose its own mode of compression, because it becomes unhinged from the 'auto-position of philosophical decision',[1] and as such from the authority of aesthetic judgment. But what does it mean for art to relinquish aesthetic judgment?

The transcendental schema of modern philosophy sets the scene for aesthetic judgment in terms of the analytic and synthetic methods of the intelligible and sensible relation to the world, the mode of self-understanding and self-feeling of the world that is described as 'human'. If this is the case, one must therefore conclude, as Denise Ferreira da Silva explains, that the sensible is the condition of affectability that defines the limit of apprehension—that is, the limit of transcendental judgment as it encounters contingency qua indeterminacy.[2] It is at this limit point that aesthetic judgment is called upon to define the conditions that allow contingency to coincide with unknowns that must and yet cannot be decided in advance. In other words, aesthetic judgment performs a negation of the negative or the unknown by subjecting it to patterns of recognition. It is here that the sensible, as da Silva argues, comes to enfold within aesthetic judgment a necessary racialization, gendering, and sexualization of the unknown as exteriorities (objects, things, worlds) in relation to the recursive constitution of the self-reflective system. Such exteriorities have no purpose and lack a teleological program (i.e., they have no inherent final form), so they can be affected but cannot affect; they can be known, but cannot know. Exteriorities serve aesthetic judgment by allowing it to distinguish the process of the abstraction/extraction of affectabilities from the formation of the autopoietic interiority of the system. This is the process that sustains racial capital insofar as the self-reflective system (self)-posits its own ontological conditions by transforming the enslaved, dispossessed exteriority into a commodity form. In so far as aesthetic judgment acts at the limit of reason, it gives a value to the void—the racialized, gendered, and sexualized empty set—that is represented as a subliminal unknown. As such, the transcendental schema reserves for art the task of accounting for the epistemological limit that marks the edge of the sublime, the point at which the problem of contingency comes to shape both the role of reason and its crisis. In other words, aesthetic judgment sustains the recursive function for the abstraction/extraction of contingencies, of that which is not yet known in the symbolic exchange of a language that can supposedly explain everything. One cannot deny that the role of the sublime for art is to both determine and relativize the historico-epistemological order of know-hows and techno-practices. As on a moebius strip, the sublime, demarcating contingency as indeterminacy, is already curved inside the loop of philosophical decision which sets up the excluded exterior as the necessary aleatory value, the non-human flesh that must be converted into a seamless thing, an instrument, a medium, a machine that serves to preserve Man's interiority. The question for the non-aesthetic is therefore how to withdraw from this circuit of authority that places art in the service of instrumental reason, for which a medium seems to embody the split between intelligible concepts and sensible objects. The medium coincides with this split, which transcendental reason must continuously synthesize in order to maintain the systemic structure of colonial, patriarchal, and racial capital.

Instead of entering art via the schema of aesthetics, art must rather offer possibilities for overturning aesthetic judgment, the authority of concepts, and the sublation of objects. Art has its own mode of compression, through which it can account for real alterity in which unknown conditions demarcate the outer limits of philosophical categories, aesthetic synthesis, and computational programming. What these limits offer, one can argue, is alien(ated) mediation resulting from the irreversible compression of noise-information. This is not so much a conversion of noise into a recognized pattern as in self-reflective analytics, or the manifestation of an aleatory event into perception. Instead, for art to refuse transcendental axiomatics, it must account for the abstraction of unpatterned randomness that runs through and against the wholeness/completeness of the system. Nevertheless, in order to withdraw from aesthetic judgment, where the sublime defines the empty space of indeterminacy as racialized, gendered, and sexualized, it is not that art must renounce abstraction in favor of an affective immediacy of experience. Instead, abstraction becomes above all synthetic or artificial: just as matter-form is already abstracted in know-how, so too techne or procedures generate matter-form abstractions, trans-models, alien forms. But what kind of matter-form should one concern oneself with in order to give an account of real alterity when talking about techno-oriented art? If the task of aesthetic judgment is to re-place indeterminacies with transcendental categories that define the role of objects, can know-how such as automated procedures, learning algorithms, and AI logic expose incompleteness in formal systems and the alienness/alienation of matter-form? Is there a non-aesthetic form in algorithmic procedures in which information exposes an alien materiality which overlaps with but is not identical to thermodynamic energy and physical matter? To answer these questions, it must first be noted that the materiality of information is not exhausted by the scientific qualities of physics, and cannot be categorized by the world of philosophical decision. Non-aesthetic art would rather address a materiality that brings forth its own abstractions, even if these are manifested as instrumentalities such as automations, procedures, synthetic methods, algorithms and AI. Instrumentalities have the advantage of a process-led mode of abstraction minus the authority of the auto-decisional model of philosophy and its aesthetic reification in the art form. In particular, information as instrumentality will grant neither transparent (self-determined) access to the ineffable real nor an encompassing immersion in the commodification of the sensible (the affectable). Adorno's negative dialectics may help to clarify this point further.[3] Adorno takes the preponderance of the object in exchange value to expose a contradiction in capital: the object—resulting from the objectification/alienation/instrumentalization of flesh into a commodity—rather asserts itself against the sublation which the autopoietic structure sets in place to justify the ever-present role of the concept and the subject. Paradoxically, the dominance of the object in the system of exchange value precisely exposes the non-identity (and the irreconcilable reality) of the object with the subject: since the commodity unleashes its objectified reality, it exposes a rupture in the synthesis of aesthetic judgment.

One could argue that the non-aesthetic instrumentality of the object turns against (or overturns) the capital program of extraction/abstraction precisely by following the negative negation of the logic of commodity exchange. Since the materiality of the object is also an instrumental form, it is materiality as a medium-form that breaks into and breaks down the autopoietic circuits of capital, language, and symbolic meaning. But how do these contradictions of instrumentality come about? Just as alien(ated) materialities become instrumental procedures for the capital form of symbolic exchange, so their automation describes a way to "transmute" (i.e. change across) matter into information—that is, to trans-mediate the limit of reason not into the sublimation/sublation of the unknown but as the alterity of incomputable forms. Similarly, Fred Moten discusses this negative abstraction as a metamorphic procedure of the enslaved flesh into a commodity fetish.[4] While abstraction/extraction requires the negation of the object (as a brutal subjection to the capital form), it also encounters the negative (or 'appositional') eruptions resulting from the very process of instrumentality (or automation) of the enslaved. Instrumentalities are therefore also insurgencies that trans-mediate information with unpredictability, signal with noise, patterns with randomness, computation with incomputabilities. Negative dialectics exposes the non-purity of information just as the negation of the object coincides with noise-information, namely as that which carries through or bears within it the textures (or infinite variations) of uncertainty, indeterminacy, randomness.

But what exactly can these textures of uncertainty do for non-aesthetic instrumentality, how can they help challenge the sublimation of the absolute unknown-flesh? It is possible to suggest that the uncertainty of results, the indeterminacy of conditions, and the randomness of patterns are entangled with the notion of noise, which entails a negative operation of recognition. For instance, the role of noise is central to machine learning, where algorithms train on data which is not already known or programmed as memory. Here the role of noise is generative insofar as it entails that algorithms learn from the differential patterns of information that noise carries. Noise does not define a point of absolute unknownness, and is not without structure or pattern, but is necessary to the automation of learning insofar as the retrieval of indeterminate variations makes it possible for algorithms to differentiate their capacity for decision-making, including recommendations that offer more than one possible outcome or probability. In other words, learning from noise expands the horizon of machine thinking insofar as, importantly, the uncertainty of results allows the system to adapt to patterns that exist but that cannot be recognized according to given schemas. In recent models of machine learning for AI vision, the addition of noisy patterns for image recognition has introduced the possibility of retrieving as many differential variations as possible in the generation of representations of subjects, objects, experiences, worlds that do not exist.[5]

Similarly, in Hecker's *Resynthesizers*, the investigation of noise opens up to a mode of machine learning for sound objects that cannot be heard or simply categorized as absolute randomness, but that nonetheless contain information and expose new conditions of possibility for listening. In particular, Hecker focuses on the texture synthesis algorithm developed by Axel Röbel and members of the Analysis/Synthesis team at IRCAM (Paris), in order to gather a variation of repetitive sound elements that are accompanied by irregular patterns and elements of noise including the duration of the sound, its acoustic frequency, and modulation frequency. However, rather than the prototypical texture sounds that feature in audiological and cognitive scientific research, *Resynthesizers* uses already synthetic sounds produced by various types of particle synthesis. In particular, in Hecker's experimentation with noise, the process of recognition is reversed in so far as the sonic objects are not analyzed and then recognized, but rather the texture analysis becomes generative of new units of sound. The algorithm featured in *Resynthesizers* processes these units through a Fourier transform—an operation that changes the domain of a signal from time to frequency—so that each local object becomes the result of the accumulation of 'unvarying [...] waves of infinite coherence'.[6] Here the asymmetry between time and synthesis domain exposes how information is always lost in one direction or the other. Noise variations come to coincide with utterances standing for incomprehensible sounds cutting across scales and generating meanings that become amplified across domains.

That noise exposes 'appositional' utterance and response is what Moten addresses when he discusses Frederick Douglas's account of Aunt Hester's scream as an instance of the infinite material variations of noise-objects that at once disrupt and expose the spectacle of black suffering. In this account, the noise-scream becomes differentially appositional to the performance of violence—'[t]he louder she screamed, the harder he whipped'[7]—as the utterances of a brutally negated/negative dispossessed affectability of non-being. Here what is classified as an absolute unknown, an apparently meaningless and unstructured noise, runs up against the brutality of the master grammar to which the scream of the flesh must be subjected in order to ensure the social performance of the equation of value. For Moten, the scream is a disturbance, 'a radically exterior orality'[8] that defies the order of the symbolic form that would rather place noise-scream outside the system of signification. Moten instead shows how this scream becomes generative of noise variations across scales. The scream returns in the Free Jazz recording performance 'Protest',[9] where Aunt Hester's scream rather becomes an instrumentality-form, a sonic object or a 'phonic materiality'.[10] In this way, the brutality of negation also brings with it the noise-information of non-origin, or the generation of matter-form as information-noise, carried over as a non-aesthetic instrumentality that has little to do with perception and recognition, but owes everything to the alien(ated) commodities whose scream pierces through the recursive logic of capital abstraction/extraction.

Instrumentality here does not just ensure that the signal passes through the channels of information communication technologies, which must compress and extract the indeterminacy of noise. Instead, it shows us that extraction does not occur with the alien(ation) of the scream qua the negated excluded fighting against the completeness of the symbolic system. Instead, the manifest image of negative abstraction does not simply define the crisis of philosophy but rather the irreversible route of 'non-philosophy':[11] the unprogrammed cloning of the real entering, erupting, and taking over self-determined thought. Here noise demarcates not the absolute indeterminacies of the sublime as the noumena standing beyond the limit of a complete system, or the incalculable standing beyond epistemology. Instead, instrumentality in the form of noise-information coincides with the objection that alien(ated) matter-form poses to the recursive function of capitalist, racial, patriarchal abstraction. It is because noise demarcates the fallibility of the autopoietic system in every act of compression (understanding, analysis, synthesis) that one can follow the persistence of noise-information not only in symbolic forms and languages, but also in generative AI.

Inasmuch as a non-aesthetic approach must account for how real alterity disrupts the epistemological paradigms of transcendental analysis and synthesis, the separation between information and noise must be also challenged. Cecile Malaspina suggests that an epistemology of noise is possible: noise stands neither for the unknowable nor for a given probability.[12] Asking '[h]ow does knowledge constitute itself in the face of contingency?', Malaspina turns to Claude Shannon's mathematical theory of communication, in which information is aligned with unpredictability and which, as such, places the principle of uncertainty at the core of epistemology. Here information is already entropy. Shannon's theory entails that certainty always implies a lack of information. From this standpoint, incompleteness becomes the causal form of the real. Malaspina argues that this contradiction between noise and information applies across disciplines, from cybernetics to psychology, from computation to cognition. Similarly, this unresolvable contradiction shows that the complex articulation of noise as exteriority or as fugitive cannot be fully subjected to the dyadic form of epistemology for which noise must play the role of the excluded/included in the articulation of structures (linguistic, psychic, economic, semiotic, etc.). Malaspina rather suggests that there is nothing natural or physically given in this information-oriented mode of noise. While noise becomes the empty set that enters political judgment, it also has a material form coinciding with 'the noise of cognition constituting itself, against the always looming crisis of its dissolution'.[13] In this sense, knowledge is neither predictable nor ultimately fallacious. It is rather a process-oriented practice of thinking that sets out from the stance of uncertainty. Knowledge is *of* uncertainty. It occupies the stance of what Laruelle calls the '[s]tranger in flesh and blood'.[14] Starting from information-noise, the extension of epistemology can be said to also entail the extension of cognition. This is not a prosthesis—the extension of the self-determining racial, patriarchal capital for which entropy, the measure of noise, must turn into a probability of and for extraction. This prosthetic extension aims to define how noise must become a negentropic instrumentality, which requires the transformation of noise into useful information: a teleological affair. As opposed to the negentropic model of self-organization, Malaspina speaks of the 'negation of the negation of contingency',[15] exposing how noise is central to meaningful yet incomplete forms. As opposed to aesthetic judgment, which places noise at the edge of the world—the sublime as contingency that must be negated and negentropically sublated into the signal/value of the commodity fetish—Malaspina argues that double negation rather reveals the generative and constructive negation of order. Noise bears this double negation as an index of refusal—the refusal of the opposition between noise and information which preserves interiority in its aesthetic, cognitive, and political forms. This is yet another manifest image of a negative dialectic that suspends the binary tension between noise as entropy—as dissipative energy that threatens the system's homeostasis—

and the aesthetic judgment of noise as the most irreducible manifestation of free choice or unregulable randomness. Non-aesthetic noise instead holds onto the entropy-information conjunction, entailing an overlapping and unresolvable friction between the destruction and the construction of form, siding with the alien(ated) noise-information of incomputable thinking.

Another way to clarify why the conception of noise must hold onto this friction is to delve more deeply into the ways in which the entropy-information conjunction is still central to computational theories today. In other words, noise as art form is central to the alien intelligibility of artificial intelligence, where the capturing of noise also includes the generation of knowledge, perception and experience. According to Malaspina, Shannon's insight into information as entropy opens up the possibility of a material analysis of uncertainty that would aim to transform the conditions of knowledge. Here Shannon's conceptualization of information and entropy already tells us that, just as information is the measure of entropy, so entropy is the 'measure of one's freedom of choice'; more precisely, the quantification of entropy (as uncertainty) cannot be divorced from but is rather entangled with freedom of choice. The greater the information, the greater the uncertainty.[16] Whereas Norbert Wiener takes information to be the principle of the organization of entropy—namely negentropy—Shannon instead gives us a negative entropy insofar as noise cannot be cancelled out of information. Entropy for Wiener is not a measure of information but a measure of chaos, and as such it must be regulated, as if it were to be mastered from the inside. But Malaspina insists that the problem of decision, the moment at which noise must be separated from information patterns, becomes a philosophical and not merely a technical problem or one of functional efficacy. Shannon however did not leave the field of entropy, but rather introduced two dimensions of entropy: information entropy and noise entropy. But how can there be novelty and certainty, unknowns and synthesis at the same time?

Malaspina suggests that Shannon's paradoxical articulation transpires from a conception of information as process rather than sequence, pattern, or procedure. In so far as information is also uncertainty, it is not a given. Rather, uncertainty increases with both information and noise. From this standpoint, the condition of information-entropy that Shannon put forth is potential information and potential noise. This is an abstraction that has no ontological ground and no pretense to become a being.

Entropy-information may be a concern in electric signals, but it is also an issue when working with large numbers (from people to data, from trends to trades). Information entropy in computational theory, for instance, is not just a simulation of physics or even a conversion of physical information into algorithms (a quantification of physical dynamics). Instead, one must look at computational theory to address the configuration of entropy-information in algorithmic and generative neural networks.

To account for noise-information in computational theory, one must turn to Gregory Chaitin, who, following Alan Turing's articulation of incomputability and Claude Shannon's statistical entropy, offers a third meaning of entropy. Here the randomness of a finite string is defined as the volume of randomness in bits which is incompressible—that is, it cannot be completed by a universal program smaller than itself. Turing addressed this limit of self-determining logic in terms of the halting problem.[17] With the halting problem, Turing proved that decision problems were unsolvable. The problem of knowledge is thus turned into a problem of incomputability, according to which formal logic and axiomatic systems are destined to remain incomplete. In formal logic, the halting problem is a decision problem insofar as it is not possible to determine in advance whether or not a computer program will stop or run forever. Turing demonstrated that it is impossible to create an algorithm that solves the halting problem for all possible input pairs of a program or a Turing Machine. Chaitin takes Turing's question of the limit of computability to involve the algorithmic processing of maximally unknowable probabilities, or what he calls Ω (Omega).[18] Chaitin calls the latter 'algorithmic randomness': the rule-based processing of unknown quantities of noise-information is no longer based on statistical probabilities, but rather coincides with algorithmic complexity: the number Ω (Omega) has infinite complexity. Each bit of Ω is also a bit of complexity. Even though Ω is well-defined mathematically, its numerical value is elusive. According to Chaitin, not only is Ω incomputable (and Turing had already addressed incomputable real numbers), but more importantly here, incomputability means that the smallest program able to calculate the first *N* bits of the base-two expansion of Ω will also have *N* bits. For Chaitin, both computationally and logically, Ω is irreducible.[19]

From this standpoint, not only noise-information but also reduction-complexity seem central to the non-aesthetic matter-form of art in so far as the compression of alien(ated) patterns helps reveal the incomputability of epistemology. Similarly, by challenging the dominance of aesthetic judgment, the epistemology of noise/randomness/incomputabilities steps beyond the self-decisional model that establishes the limits of knowledge as we know it.

Florian Hecker's *Resynthesizers* is not a sublimation of noise. It does not relinquish the complexity of its components to the contemplation of indeterminacy. Instead of a transcendental synthesis, we have here a synthetic—i.e., artificial—juxtaposition of sound textures and sonic tonalites, textual and e-ink elements, along with the engineered molecules of perfumes. While speakers, scent diffusers, and e-ink displays sit together in Schindler's L-shaped Californian house, *Resynthesizers* holds these elements together as if they were ruptures in the topologically continuous experience of the sensible. The psycho-computational variations of noise-information at each and every level of analysis are not conflated in a common source of emission. Instead, the components maintain a spatio-temporal discreteness in their repetitive sonic and olfactory patterns whose iterative functions take over the interior of the house as they route around its shape. Similarly, noise-information here cannot be portioned out and then reassembled by visitors. What happens is the other way around: visitors encounter noise-information objects as they overlap and conjugate across the space-time that they traverse. It is as if maximally unknowable probabilities come to open up a field of synthetic or artificial perception (audio-visual-olfactory orientation of a synthetic sensible) that has no subject, but only instrumental mediation. Here, as much as machine listening brings forth the analytic quantification of the world in objects (sound-objects, texts-objects, smell-objects, spatial-objects), it also programs the experience of these objects in the trans-mediatic processing of technical mentalities. This is not a matter of recognizing sonic particles and scent molecules. Rather, *Resynthesizers* foregrounds the non-standard techno-scientific principles of randomness, non-linearity, complexity, incomputabilities, incompressibility, and incompleteness: a non-aesthetic transmission of noise-information that constantly undoes the program of transcendence. For instance, machine listening here coincides with how the sound textures can enter the auditory system and become components of a synthetic process which employs artificial listening agents. In the exhibition, these agents enter in a listening conversation. Instead of placing Artificial Intelligence in the role of composer or performer, in *Resynthesizers*, artificially generated sounds enter into a dialogical condition where the complexity of sounds and the computational procedures that generate them come to manifest an artificial semiotics that renders noise patterns audible. In other words, *Resynthesizers*' particle analysis and synthesis extends the field of listening: it affords the tracing of the 'non-human brain-ear' of machines.

Hecker's *Resynthesizers* demarcates an important new step in his long-term experimentation with the synthetic form of sound textures. The tension between randomness and signal or noise and information is central to Josh McDermott's statistical study of the parametric description of visual textures, which Hecker employed in the work *Affordance* (2013).[20] The modeling of a base sound signal in McDermott's work entails an iterative optimization of noise whereby the original texture is extracted from a set of parameters, to then create a sound using the same parameters.[21] Importantly, the sound produced is not simply a copy, but has the same textural properties as the original sound. What takes place between one parameter and another, however, entails a texture loss, or in other words noise, which comes to demarcate the distance between the parameters of a given sound and those of the original texture, in terms of information. Hecker's study of the perception of sound texture led to a new parametric representation of sounds, allowing for the imposition of perceptually relevant sets of parameters into noise or—more experimentally— other arbitrary input sounds. Hecker developed these statistical descriptors of sounds through noise-like signals produced with an adaptation of Xenakis's GENDYN algorithm.[22] The set of resynthesized versions, called *Resynthese FAVN,* was presented in Hecker's exhibition *Halluzination, Perspektive, Synthese*.[23] But this study of cognitive findings about what sonic noise may sound like acquires a nuanced tendency with *Resynthesizers*, which uses an entirely novel approach which differs from the code that Axel Röbel et al. had previously developed for *Resynthese FAVN*. As in deep convolutional neural networks, central to machine vision and speech models of sound generation and recognition, sound here is stochastically synthesized. By starting with a random hypothesis or guess (coinciding with a Brownian motion noise), algorithms add a corrective term to the signal at every iteration in order to match time-frequency scattering coefficients with a predefined textural target. What is new in this audio texture synthesis is the automated learning from noise variations by means of trial and error. Instead of auditory representation of noise pattern, we have here an analysis of time-frequency scattering of noise. The stochastic effects in the sampling of Brownian motion and the finiteness of computational resources allow for a correlation between signals and symbols, information-noise and computational representations. *Resynthesizers* thus open up to the artificiality of perceptual processing, capturing time frequency and time content while tracing features for multi-scale textures that trace the timbre of a sound. This computational auditory analysis defined by time-frequency entails a progressive application of the transform to generate versions of noise patterns through the iterative modulation of a patternless sonic base. *Resynthesizers* entails the noisy approximations of auditory features that are, as it were, exposed by the ear-brain of the machine. The latter becomes a listening agent that tracks temporal events that expose the transfer of noise-information across scale while transforming the experience of the auditory landscape.

Here the time-frequency scattering of noise opens up to machine sound generated events with variation rather than a classical compression of noise into information. The negation of the negation of the complex variations of noise patterns also enters into dialogue with the computational processing of incomputabilities that carry over in algorithmic procedures. In *Resynthesizers* the end result is indeterminate not because its complex tonalities are equivalent to unpatterned noise or unknowns, but because computation generates what at once could be known and is not, or, in other words, counterfactual noise-information.

But the complex tonalities of sonic objects are also in dialogue with olfactory and textual objects. Beside synthetic sound, *Resynthesizers* includes the synthetic design of scents created by Marc vom Ende and Philip Kraft. Just as artificial sound becomes the input source for the scalar generative variation of sonic patterns, so the synthetic scents reflect the combinatory amalgam of discrete variations in a continuous space. The Vanillin becomes diffused together with the antiseptic smell of the disinfected surfaces of recent Covid-19 memory, spreading through the house together with the popular molecule Calone. These engineered scents are 'accords' built around specific molecules, but are are also noise patterns for the olfactory regime insofar as they bring with them a discrete and yet non-recognizable timbre. The scents are meant to engender a series of artificial sensations which cannot be traced back to a given source but which nonetheless affect the visitor, unleashing the irregularities of perception. As much as *Resynthesizers* dramatizes the decomposition and recomposition of sonic, olfactory, and textual agents, it also exposes the negative negation of noise, whereby elements remain unidentifiable and refuse the transcendental logic of digital decision (or binary states). *Resynthesizers* exposes the discreteness of entropic breaks diffused as potential noise and potential information within the space of the exhibition. As *Resynthesizers* embraces the automation of noise, it also, as Laruelle would say, offers us a series of philo-fictions—where noise becomes alien(ated), insurgency exposing alterity as 'a full and positive void'.[24] This is a non-aesthetic zone that conditions art to stand not at the limit of reason as the sublime, but rather to side with philo-fiction, 'photo-fiction', 'music-fiction', 'smell-fiction', 'space-fiction', exposing the negative ruptures in artistic performance as much as the non-performance of artificial objects. For Laruelle, this condition of fictionality results from the method of conjugation or vectorialization of non-identical variables.[25] Instead of merging all the objects into one continuous being, *Resynthesizers* rather calls for the alterity of superpositions. What visitors are faced with as they enter *Resynthesizers*' space of discreteness is the overlapping of noise-information components, levels, layers as manifesting the negative collapse of the system—namely, of the negation of the sensible and the intelligible as we know them.

1 F. Laruelle, *Principles of Non-Philosophy*, tr. A.P. Smith (London: Bloomsbury, 2013).
2 D. Ferreira da Silva, *The Global Idea of Race* (Minneapolis: University of Minnesota Press, 2007).

3 T.W. Adorno, *Negative Dialectics*, tr. E.B. Ashton (London and New York: Routledge, 1990).

4 F. Moten, *In the Break: The Aesthetics of the Black Radical Tradition* (Minneapolis: University of Minnesota Press, 2003).

5 See for instance, the 'Random Face Generator' at <https://this-person-does-not-exist.com/en>.

6 F. Hecker and R. Mackay, 'Synthetic Listening', in F.J. Bonnet and B. Sanson (eds.), *Spectres III: Ghosts in the Machine* (Paris: Shelter Press/INA grm, 2022), 57–66: 58.

7 Ibid., 9.

8 Ibid., 6.

9 Fred Moten discusses Aunt Hester's scream as an 'appositional' utterance and response, which returns as a core component of the recording/performance called 'Protest' as part of the movement called 'free jazz' (ibid., 22).

10 Ibid.

11 Laruelle, *Principles of Non-Philosophy*.

12 C. Malaspina, *An Epistemology of Noise* (London: Bloomsbury, 2018).

13 Ibid., 173.

14 F. Laruelle, 'The Stranger as Void, Law, and Multitudo Transcendentalis: On the Concept of "Human Multitudes"', tr. J.R. Smith, <https://endemictheory.wordpress.com/2021/04/09/translation-of-francois-laruelle-the-stranger-as-void-law-and-multitudo-transcendentalis-from-theorie-des-etrangers-1995/>. (excerpted from *Théorie des étrangers: science des hommes, démocratie, non-psychanalyse* [Paris: Kimé, 1995], 159–63).

15 Malaspina, *An Epistemology of Noise*, 183.

16 Ibid., 16.

17 A. Turing, 'On Computable Numbers, with an Application to the Entscheidungsproblem', *Proc. London Math. Soc.* 2:42 (1936–7): 230–65. Reprinted in A.M. Turing, *Collected Works: Mathematical Logic*, eds. R.O. Gandy and C.E.M. Yates (Amsterdam and London: North-Holland, 2001).

18 C.S. Calude and G. Chaitin, 'What is...a Halting Probability?', *Notices of the American Mathematical Society* 57:2 (2010).

19 In 'The Limits of Reason', Chaitin sets the premises of algorithmic information theory in the context of epistemology, arguing that the pillars of knowledge can be re-envisioned from within computation. Chaitin describes the classical method of ascertaining the limits of knowledge in terms of the power of a proof to compress patternless information. His scope is to challenge the classical model of mathematics that explains reality according to an a priori decision-making whereby a theorem is validated by a proof. If a theory is simpler than the data it is supposed to explain then it is possible to establish that the theorem is a law valid for the data. But if the theory is as complex as the data it explains, not only is the theorem not a law, but the data remain lawless. Chaitin's algorithmic information theory however makes the case for the existence of an infinite number of theorems that cannot be proven by any finite system of axioms (G. Chaitin, 'The Limits of Reason', *Scientific American*, March 2006, 75).

20 *Affordance* [15 min 45 sec], 3-channel electroacoustic sound, loudspeaker system. Produced on the occasion of the exhibition *Soundings: A Contemporary Score*, Museum of Modern Art, New York, NY, USA, 10 August–3 November 2013.

21 These parameters coincide with a set of perceptually-based statistics that aim at mimicking the processing of sound textures by the human auditory system. The parameters are the cross-correlations between the feature map of a trained 2D Convolutional Neural Network (CNN), involving a signal possessing the same parameters as the original texture, as an optimization problem. H. Caracalla, and A. Röbel, 'Sound Texture Synthesis Using RI Spectograms', UMR STMS 9912 Sorbonne University, IRCAM, CNRS (2019), arXiv:1910.09497v1.

22 See P. Hoffmann, 'The New GENDYN Program', *Computer Music Journal* 24:2 (2000), 31–38.

23 Florian Hecker, *Halluzination, Perspektive, Synthese*, 17 November 2017–14 January 2018, Kunsthalle Wien, Vienna.

24 Laruelle, 'The Stranger as Void', 165.

25 F. Laruelle, *The Concept of Non-Photography*, tr. R. Mackay (Falmouth and New York: Urbanomic/Sequence Press, 2010).

COVARIANCE MATRICES OF CNN FEATURE ACTIVATIONS

AXEL RÖBEL

COVARIANCE MATRICES OF CNN FEATURE ACTIVATIONS

RESYNTHESIZERS 0.1
RESYNTHESIZERS 0.2
RESYNTHESIZERS 0.3

(FROM TOP LEFT TO BOTTOM RIGHT)

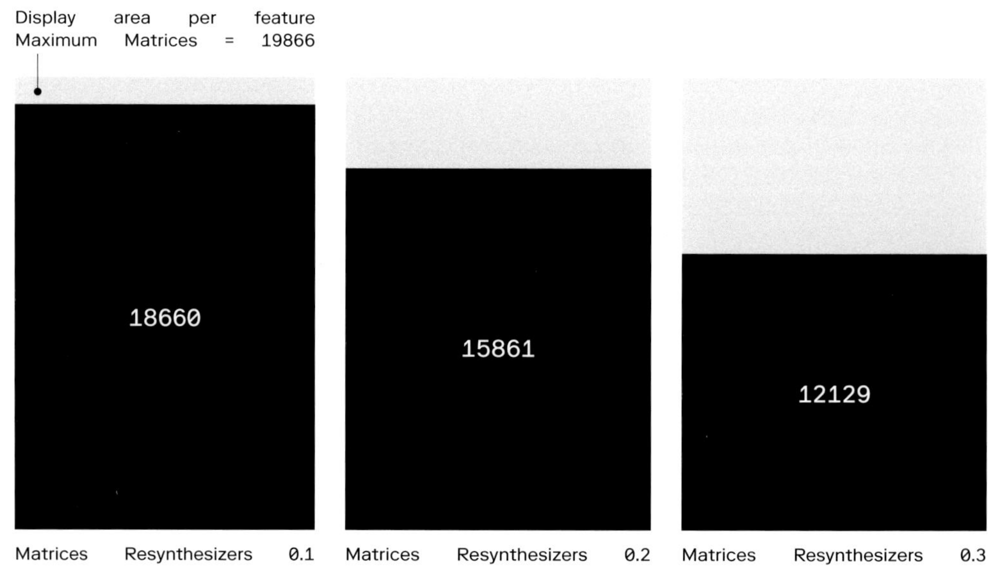

Resynthesizers	0.1
Matrices	00001-01439
Scale	1:42

Resynthesizers	0.1
Matrices	01440-03839
Scale	1:40

Resynthesizers 0.2
Matrices 00000-01040
Scale 1:40

Resynthesizers 0.3
Matrices 00000-00000
Scale 1:40

Resynthesizers 0.1
Matrices 03840–06005
Scale 1:38

Resynthesizers	0.2
Matrices	01041-03206
Scale	1:38

Resynthesizers	0.3
Matrices	00000-00000
Scale	1:38

Resynthesizers	0.1
Matrices	06006–07949
Scale	1:36

Resynthesizers	0.2
Matrices	03207-05150
Scale	1:36

Resynthesizers	0.3
Matrices	00000-01418
Scale	1:36

Resynthesizers	0.1
Matrices	07950–09683
Scale	1:34

Resynthesizers	0.2
Matrices	05151-06884
Scale	1:34

Resynthesizers 0.3
Matrices 01419-03152
Scale 1:34

Resynthesizers	0.1
Matrices	09684–11219
Scale	1:32

Resynthesizers	0.2
Matrices	06885–08420
Scale	1:32

Resynthesizers	0.3
Matrices	03153–04688
Scale	1:32

Resynthesizers	0.1
Matrices	11220-12569
Scale	1:30

Resynthesizers	0.2
Matrices	08421–09770
Scale	1:30

Resynthesizers	0.3
Matrices	04689-06038
Scale	1:30

Resynthesizers	0.1
Matrices	12570–13745
Scale	1:28

Resynthesizers 0.2
Matrices 09771–10946
Scale 1:28

Resynthesizers	0.3
Matrices	06039-07214
Scale	1:28

Resynthesizers	0.1
Matrices	13746–14759
Scale	1:26

Resynthesizers	0.2
Matrices	10947–11960
Scale	1:26

Resynthesizers 0.3
Matrices 07215–08228
Scale 1:26

Resynthesizers	0.1
Matrices	14760–15623
Scale	1:24

Resynthesizers	0.2
Matrices	11961–12824
Scale	1:24

Resynthesizers 0.3
Matrices 08229–09092
Scale 1:24

Resynthesizers	0.1
Matrices	15624–16349
Scale	1:22

Resynthesizers	0.2
Matrices	12825–13550
Scale	1:22

Resynthesizers	0.3
Matrices	09093-09818
Scale	1:22

Resynthesizers	0.1
Matrices	16350–16949
Scale	1:20

Resynthesizers	0.2
Matrices	13551–14150
Scale	1:20

Resynthesizers	0.3
Matrices	09819–10418
Scale	1:20

Resynthesizers	0.1
Matrices	16950–17435
Scale	1:18

Resynthesizers	0.2
Matrices	14151–14636
Scale	1:18

Resynthesizers 0.3
Matrices 10419–10904
Scale 1:18

Resynthesizers	0.1
Matrices	17436–17819
Scale	1:16

Resynthesizers 0.2
Matrices 14637–15020
Scale 1:16

Resynthesizers 0.3
Matrices 10905–11288
Scale 1:16

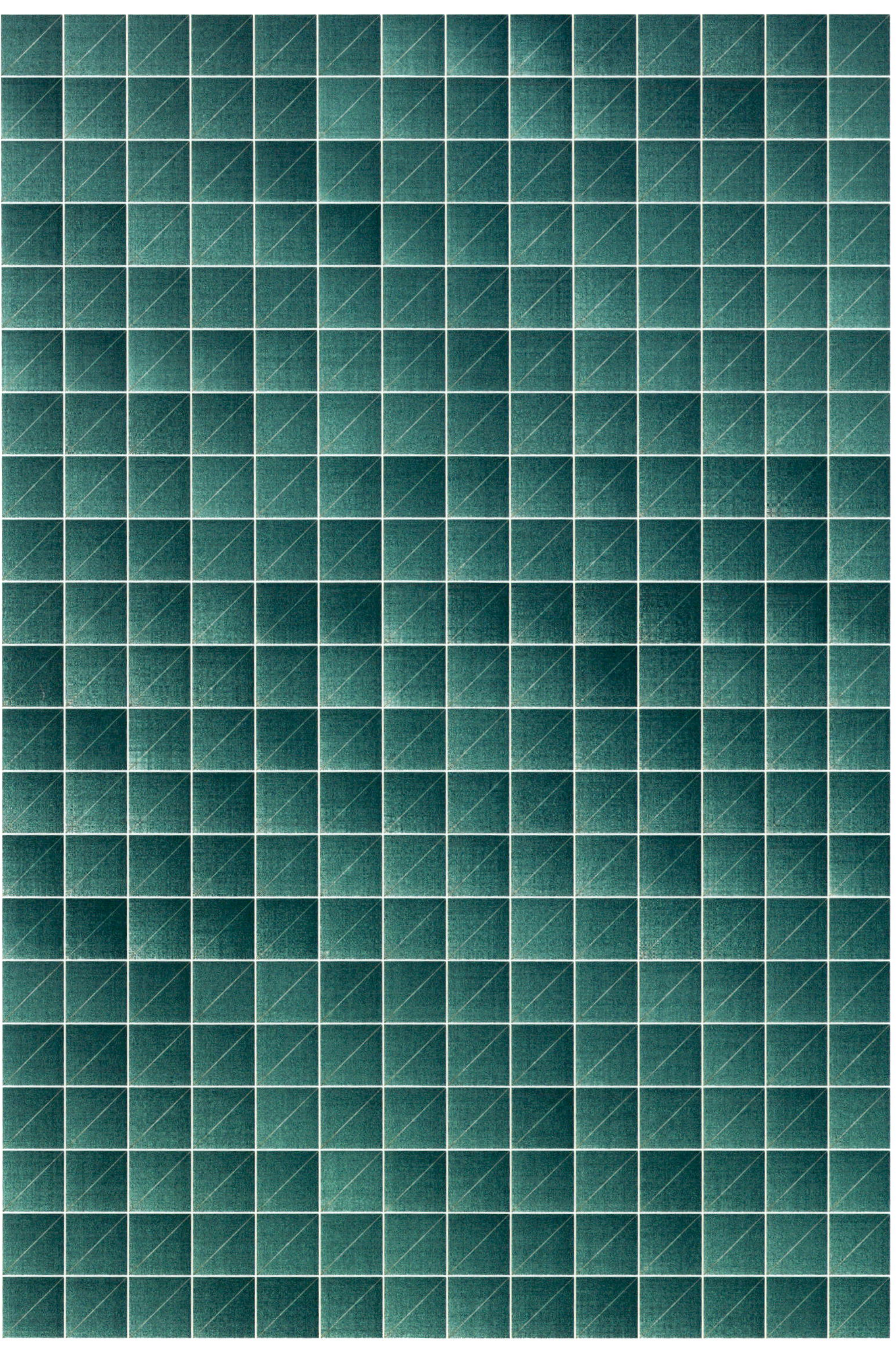

Resynthesizers 0.1
Matrices 17820–18113
Scale 1:14

Resynthesizers	0.2
Matrices	15021–15314
Scale	1:14

Resynthesizers	0.3
Matrices	11289–11582
Scale	1:14

Resynthesizers	0.1
Matrices	18114–18329
Scale	1:12

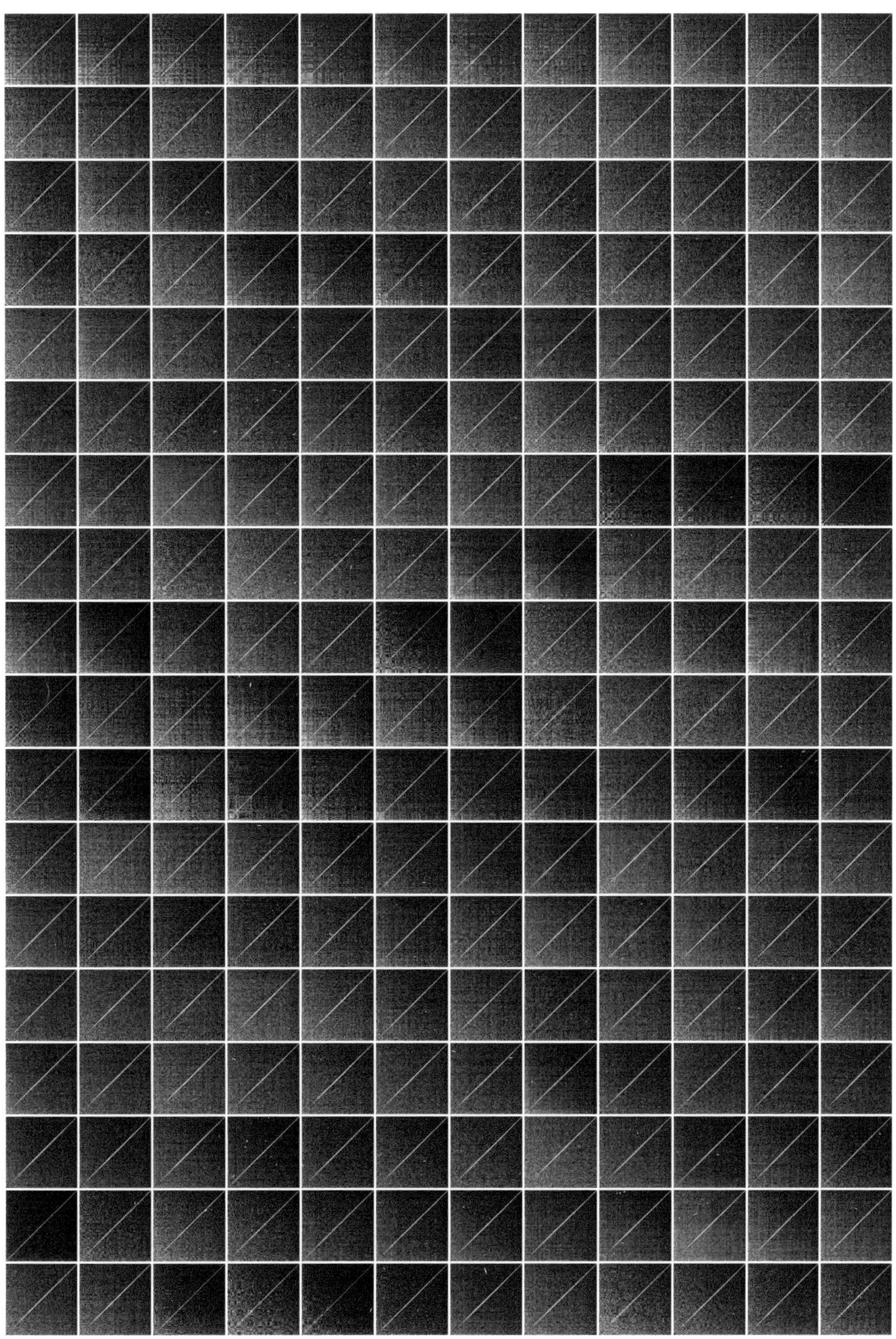

Resynthesizers	0.2
Matrices	15315–15530
Scale	1:12

Resynthesizers	0.3
Matrices	11583–11798
Scale	1:12

Resynthesizers	0.1
Matrices	18330–18479
Scale	1:10

Resynthesizers	0.2
Matrices	15531–15680
Scale	1:10

Resynthesizers	0.3
Matrices	11799–11948
Scale	1:10

Resynthesizers 0.1
Matrices 18480–18575
Scale 1:8

Resynthesizers 0.2
Matrices 15681–15776
Scale 1:8

Resynthesizers	0.3
Matrices	11949–12044
Scale	1:8

Resynthesizers	0.1
Matrices	18576–18629
Scale	1:6

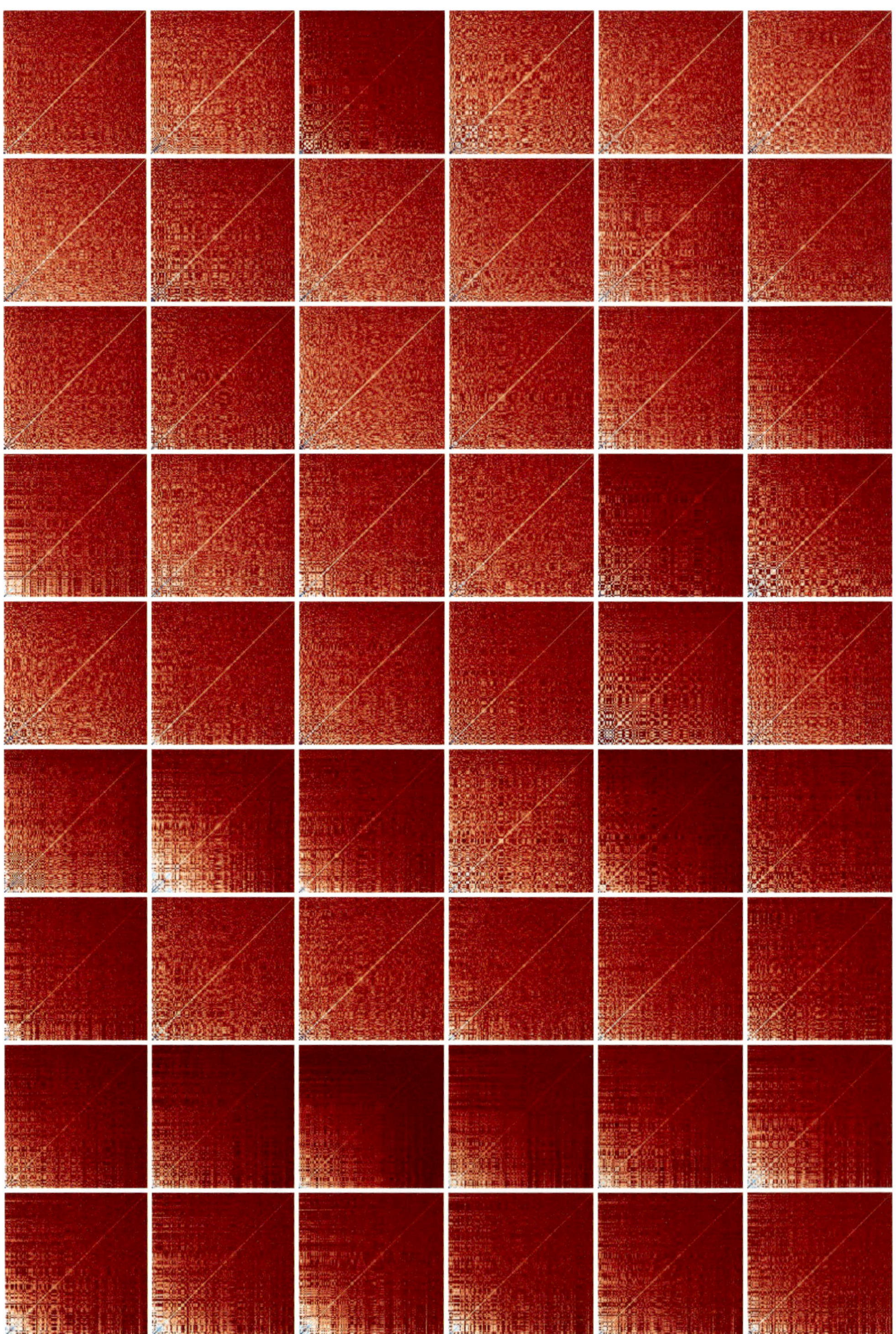

Resynthesizers	0.2
Matrices	15777–15830
Scale	1:6

Resynthesizers	0.3
Matrices	12045–12098
Scale	1:6

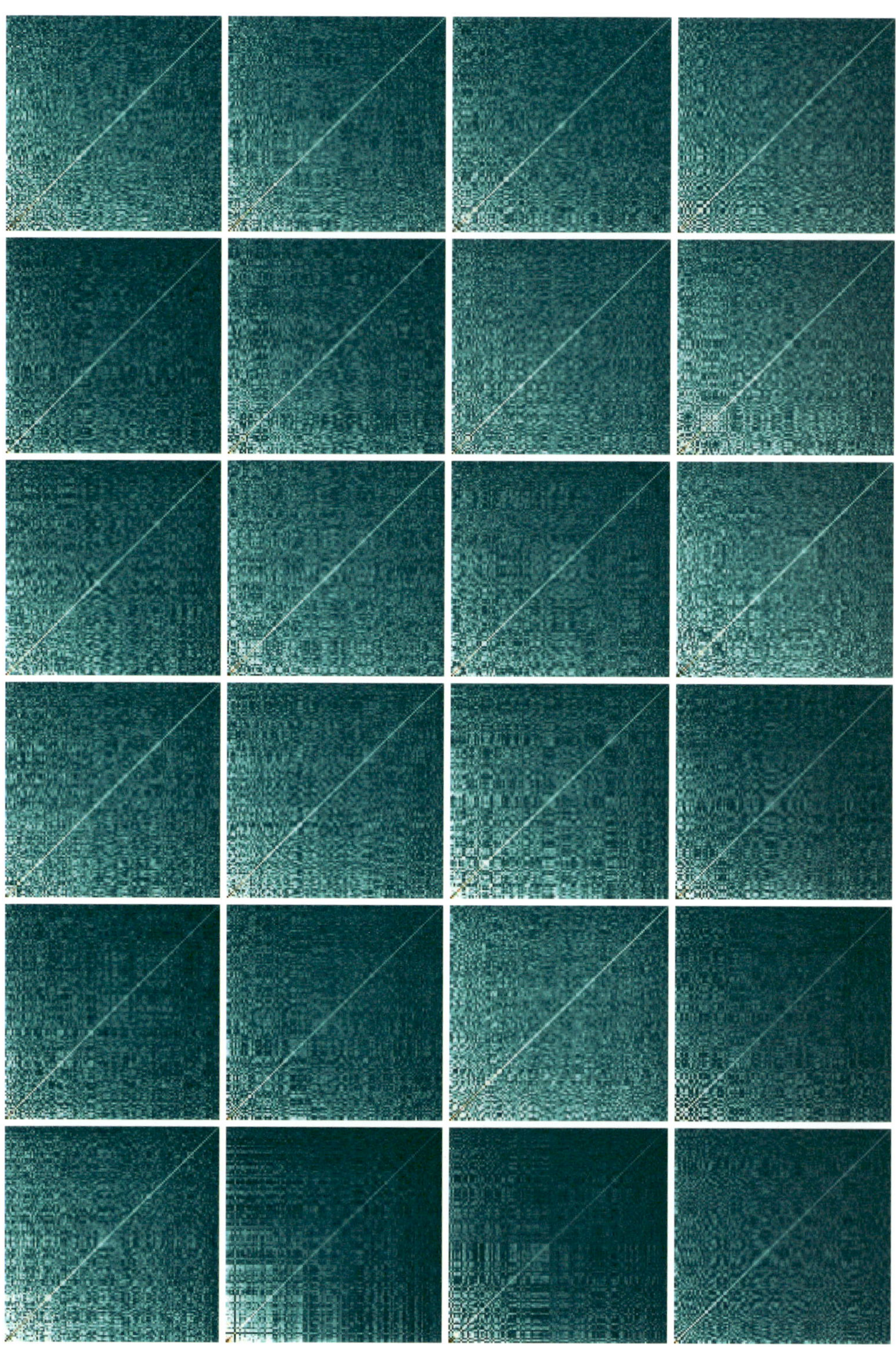

Resynthesizers	0.1
Matrices	18630–18653
Scale	1:4

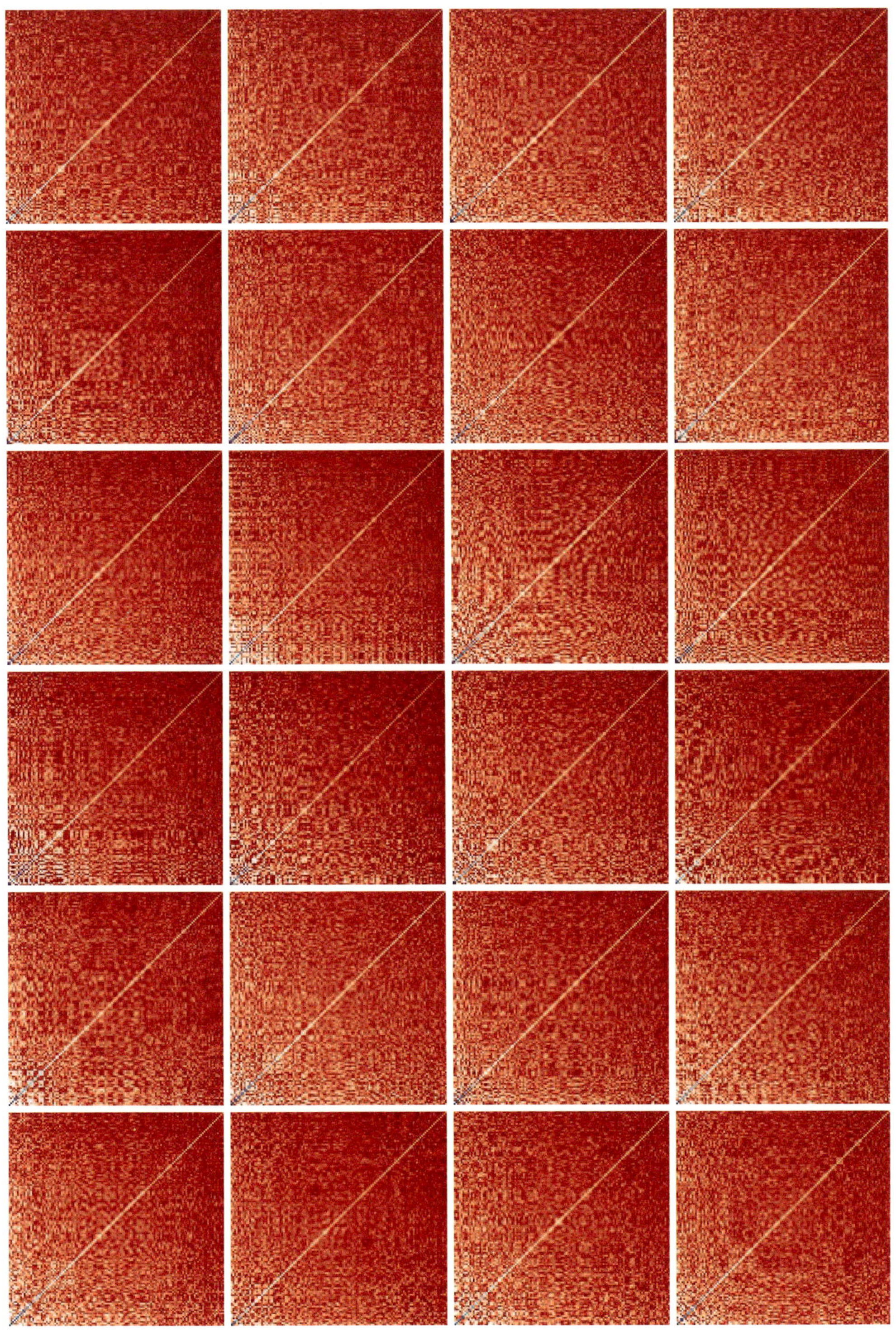

Resynthesizers	0.2
Matrices	15831–15854
Scale	1:4

Resynthesizers	0.3
Matrices	12099–12122
Scale	1:4

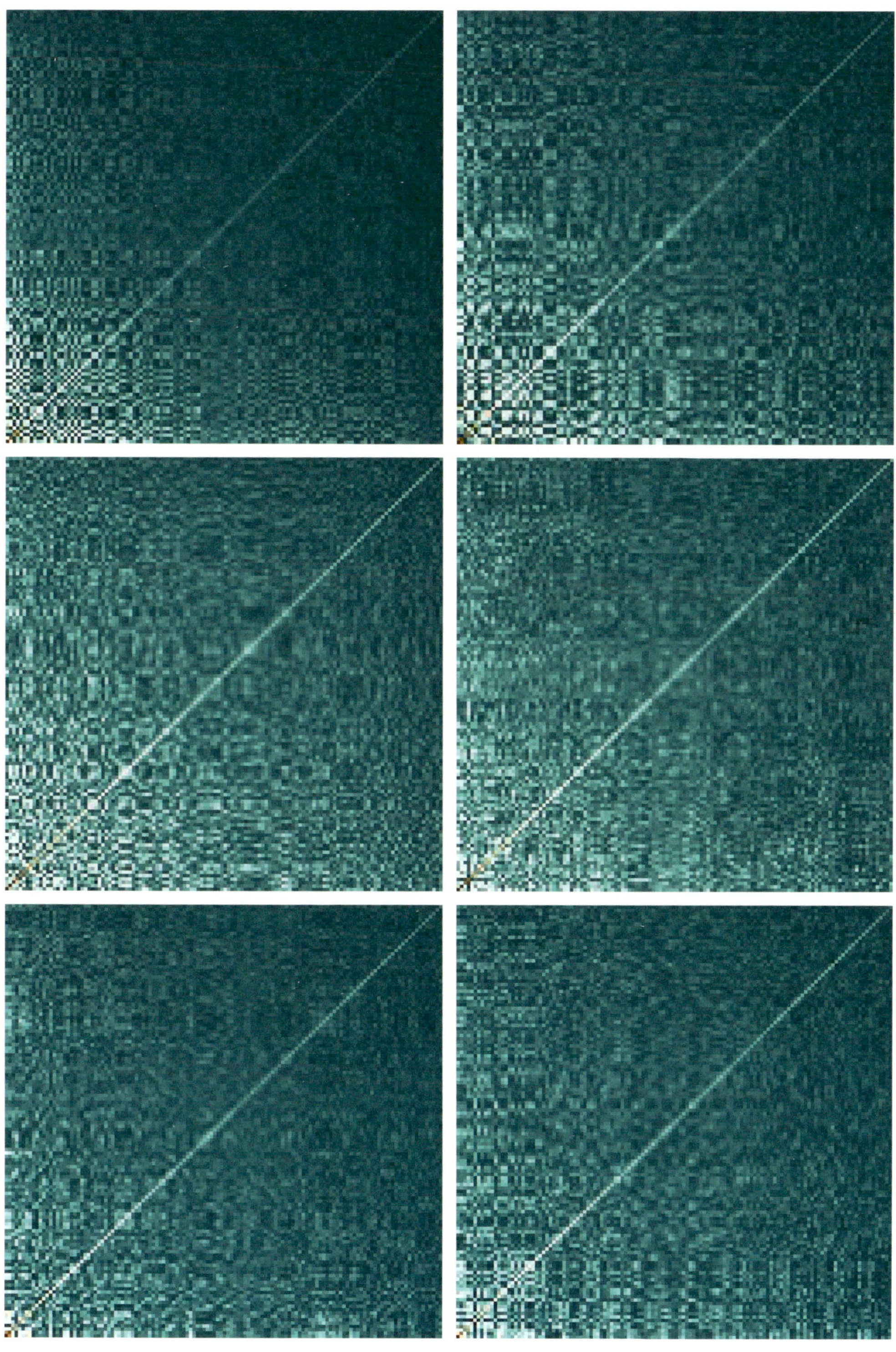

Resynthesizers	0.1
Matrices	18654–18659
Scale	1:2

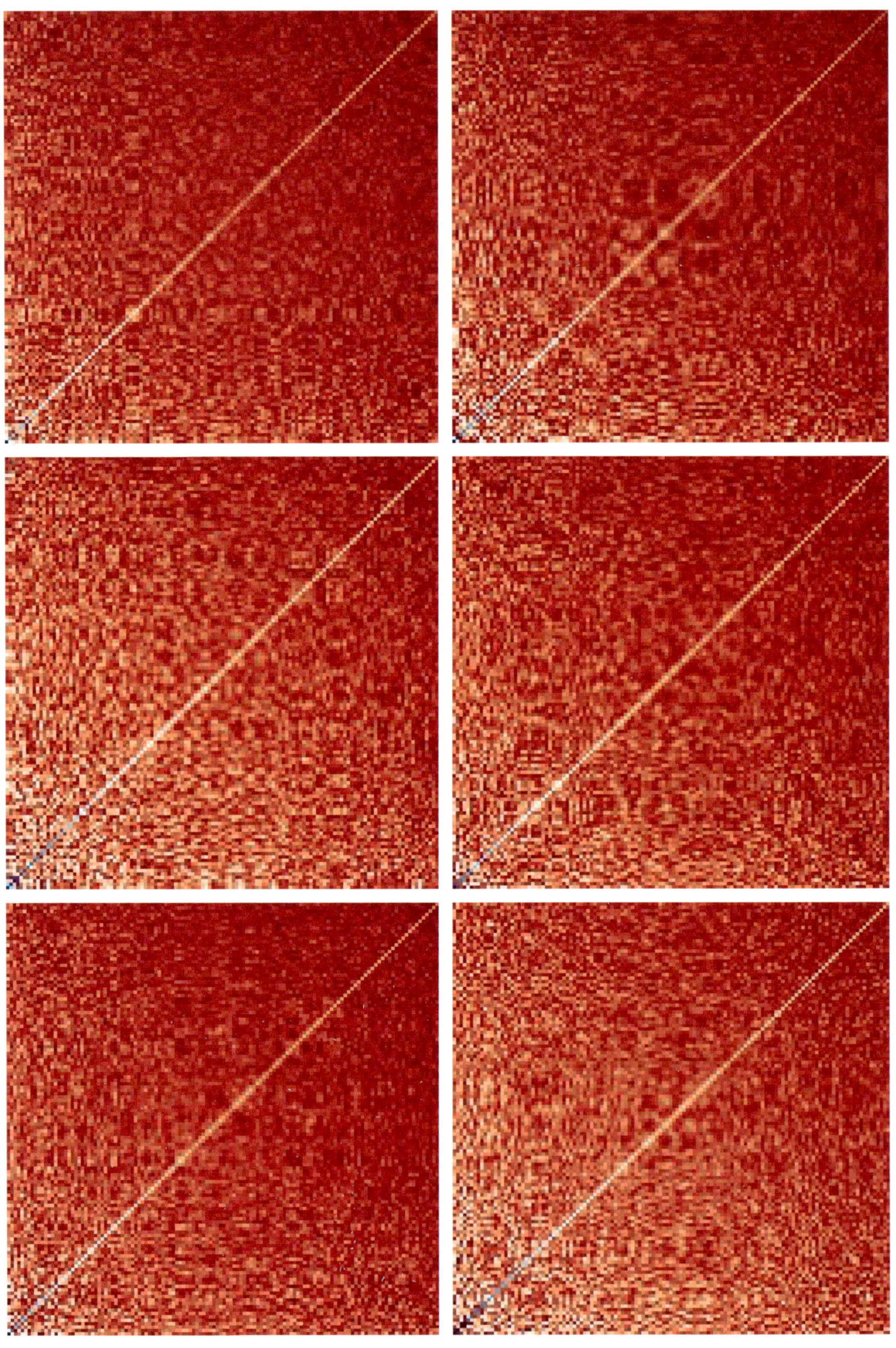

Resynthesizers 0.2
Matrices 15855–15860
Scale 1:2

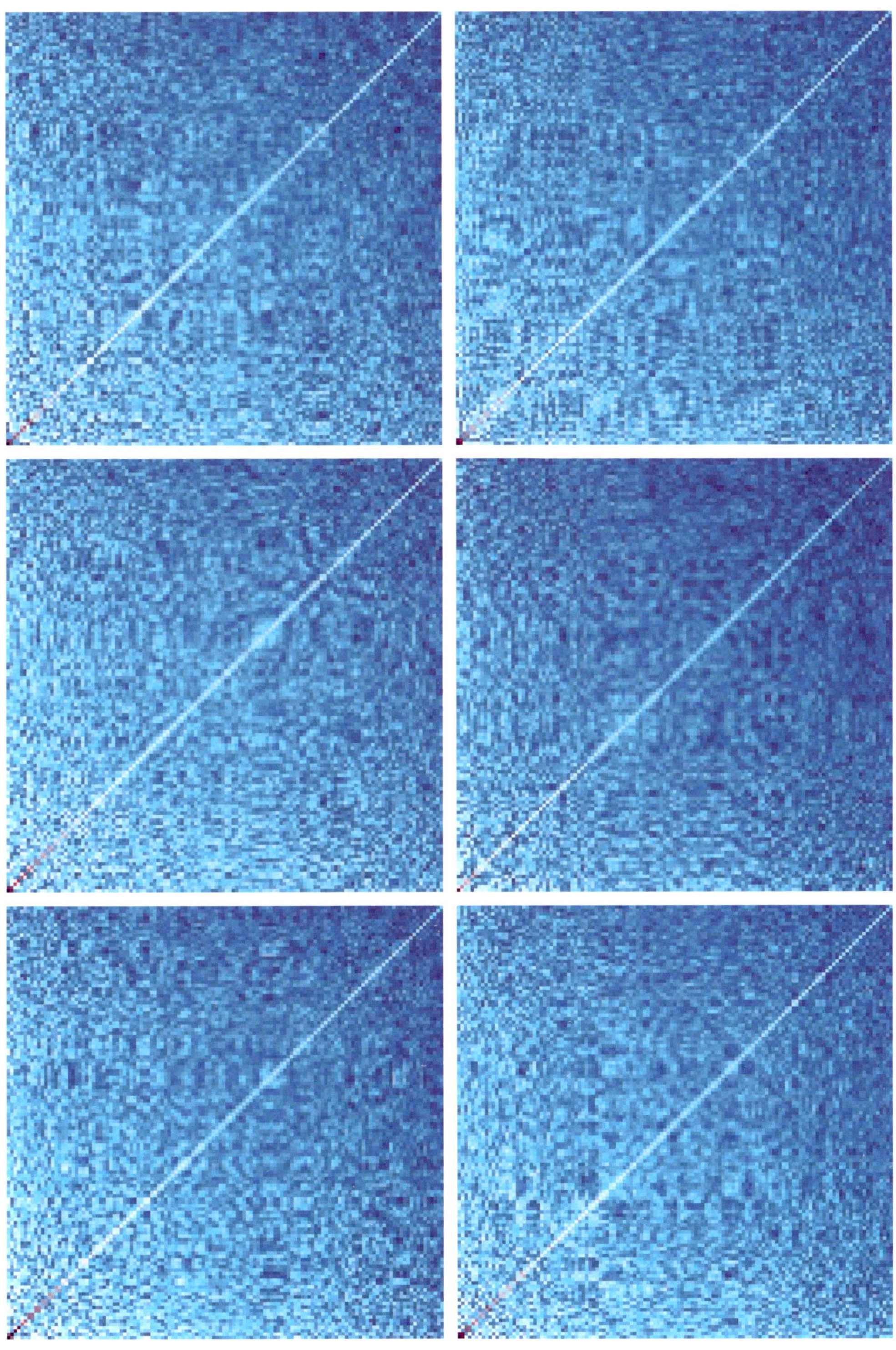

Resynthesizers	0.3
Matrices	12123–12128
Scale	1:2

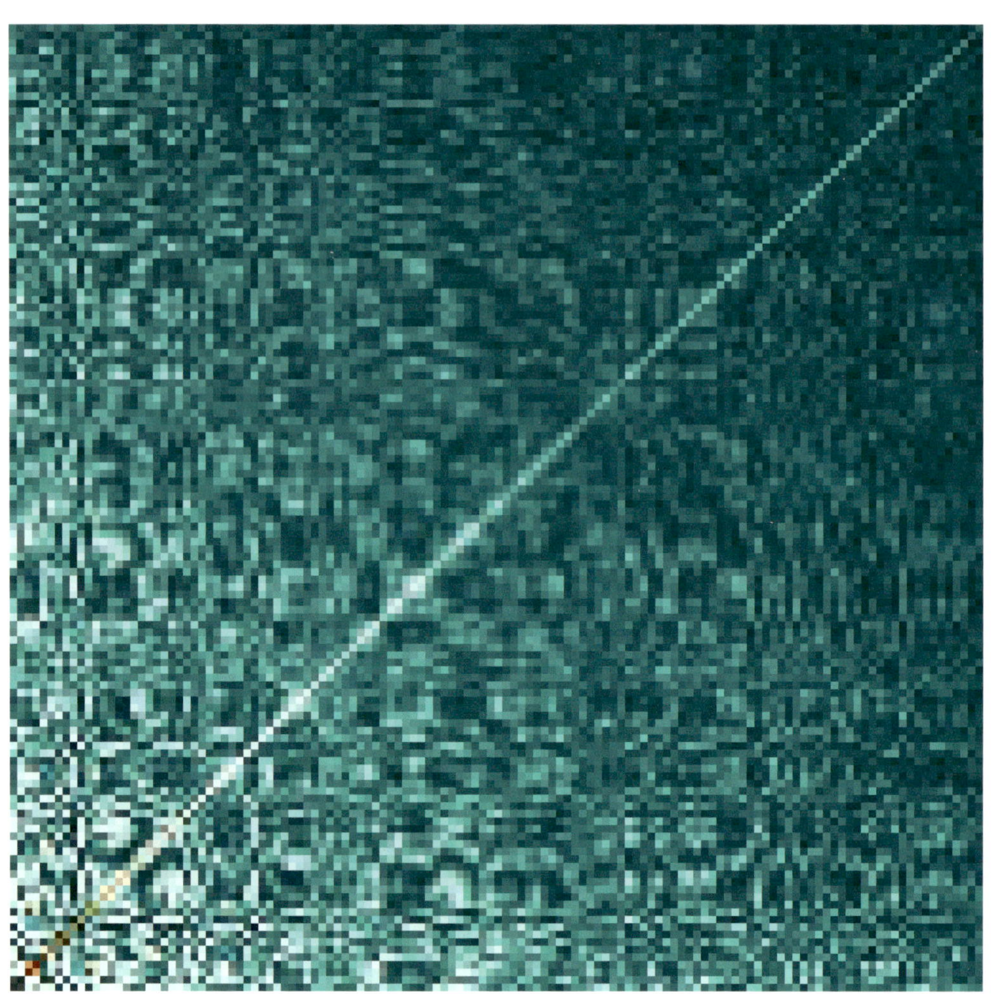

Resynthesizers	0.1
Matrice	18660
Scale	1:1

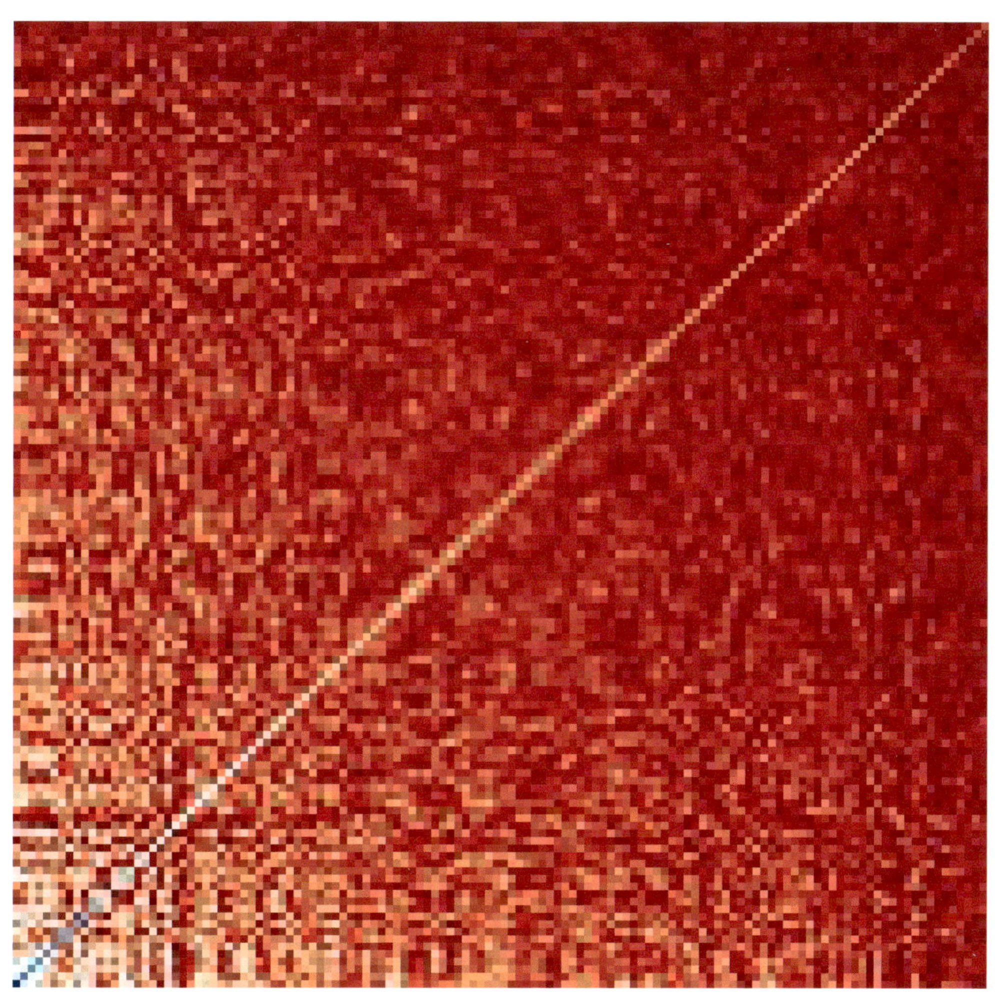

Resynthesizers 0.2
Matrice 15861
Scale 1:1

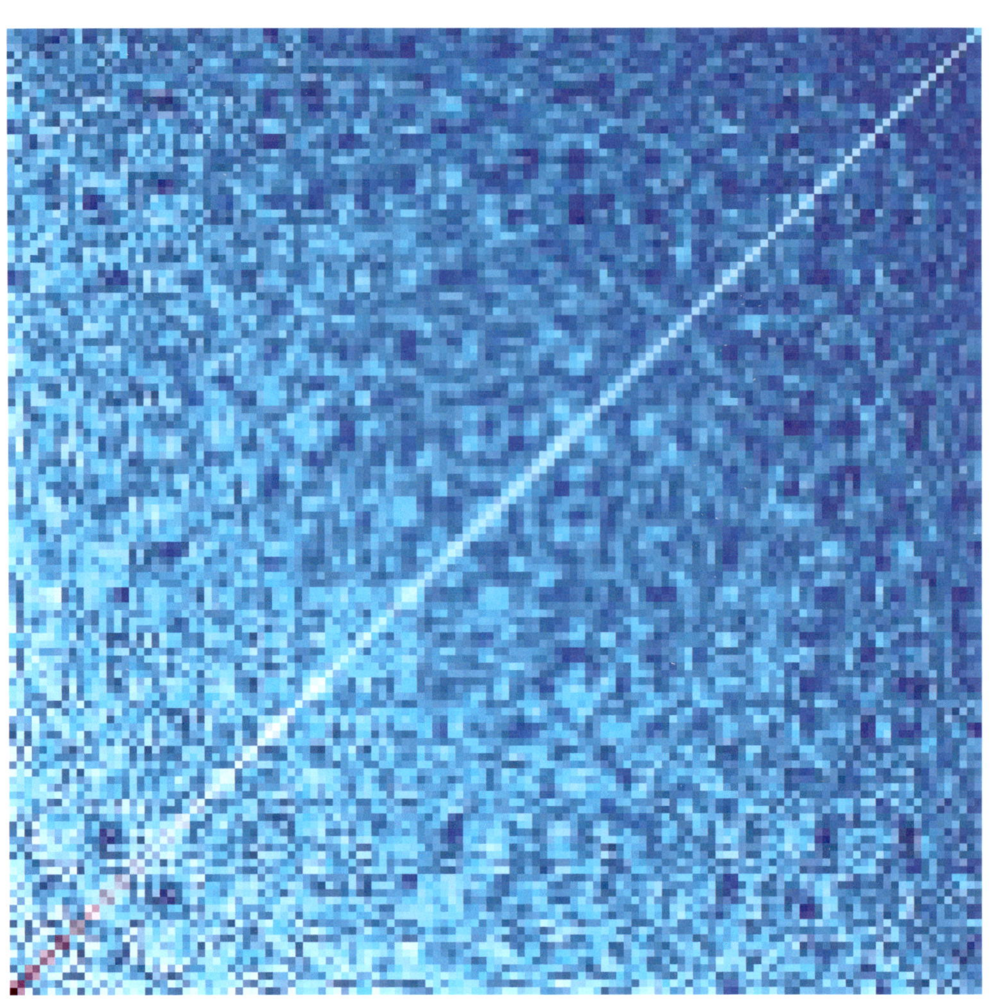

Resynthesizers	0.3
Matrice	12129
Scale	1:1

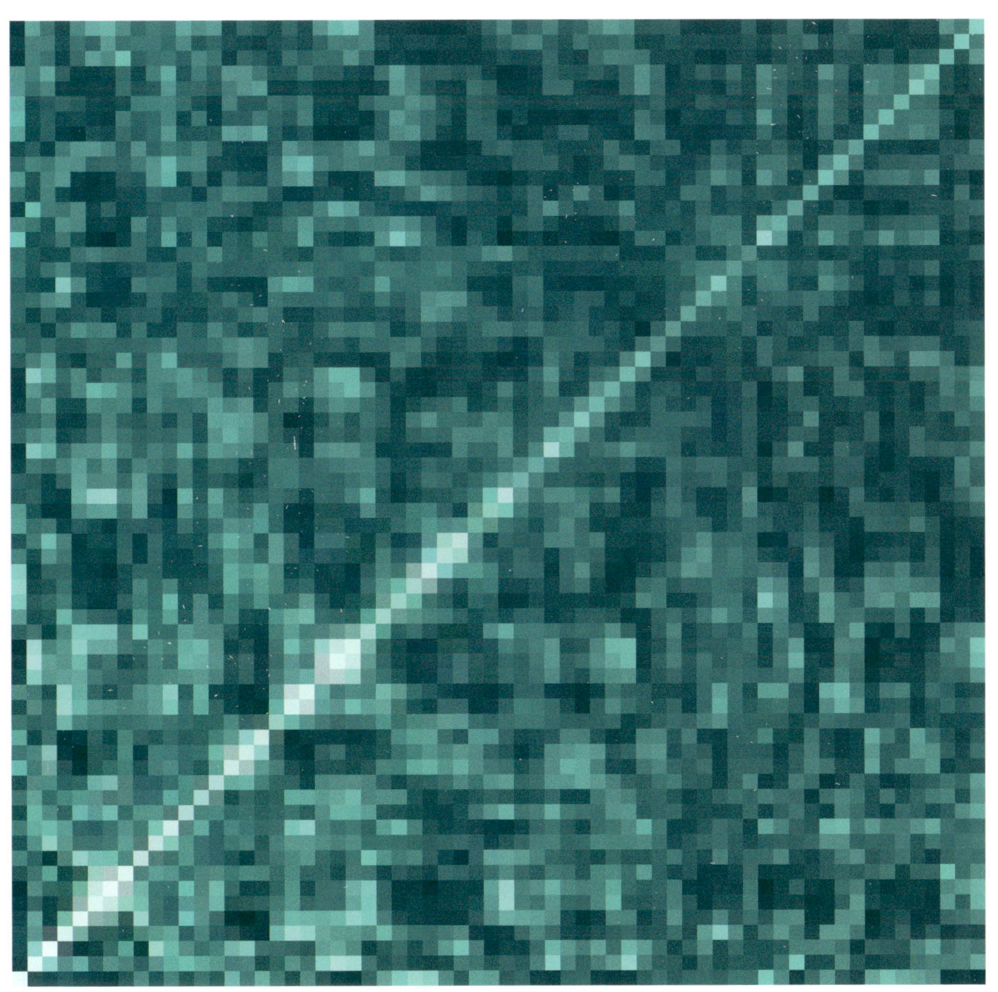

Resynthesizers	0.1
Matrice	18660
Scale	2:1

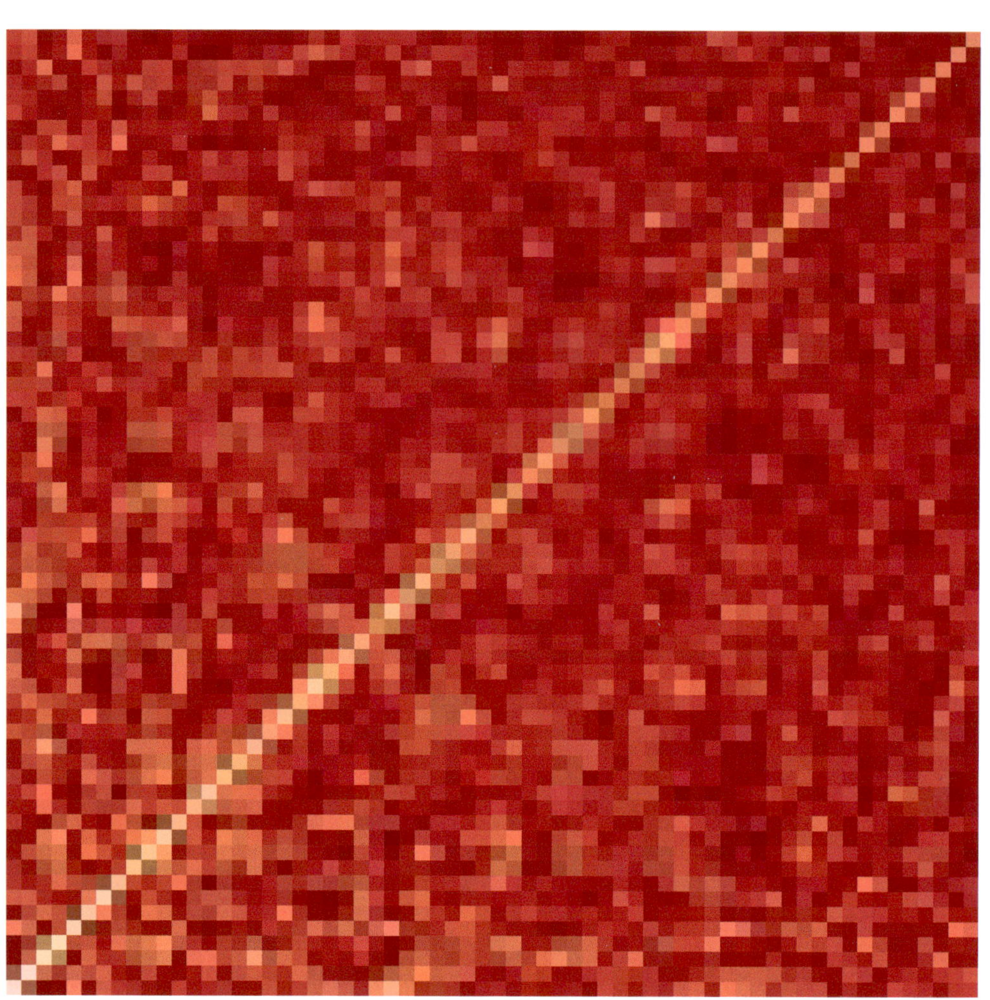

Resynthesizers	0.2
Matrice	15861
Scale	2:1

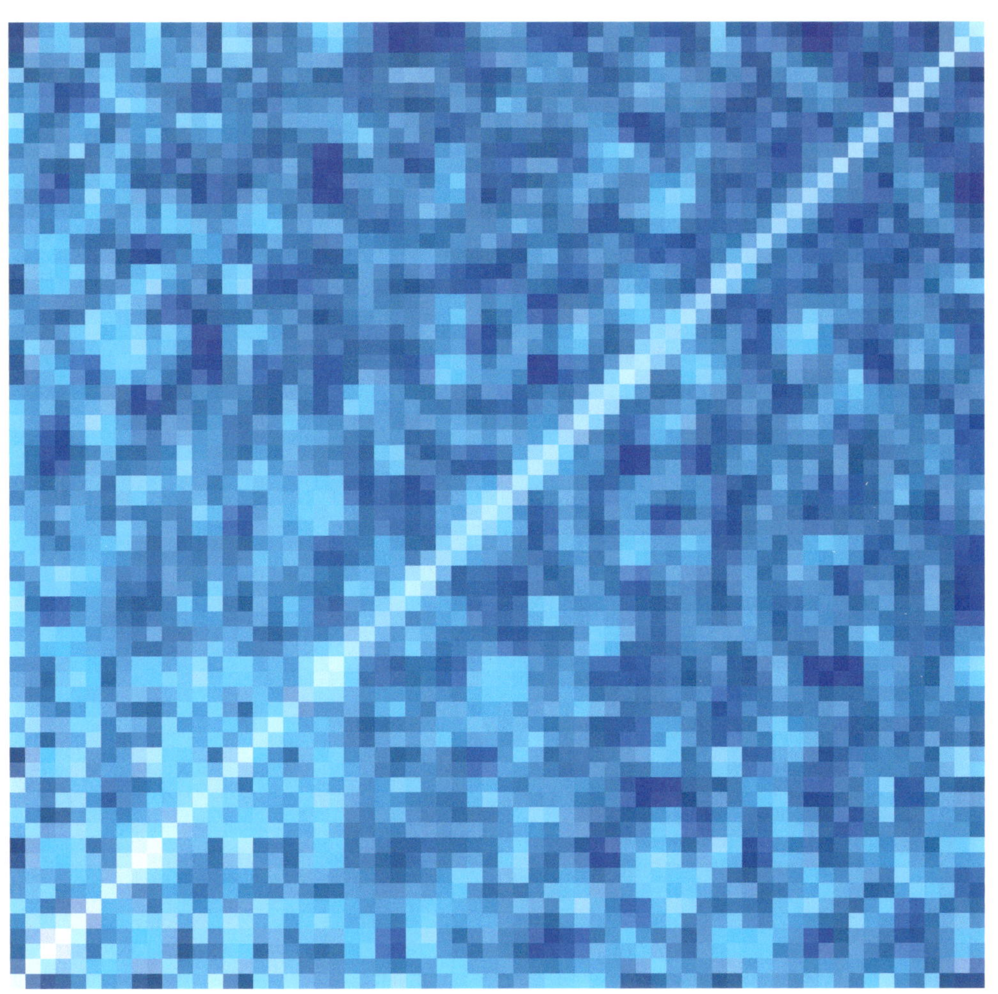

Resynthesizers	0.3
Matrice	12129
Scale	2:1

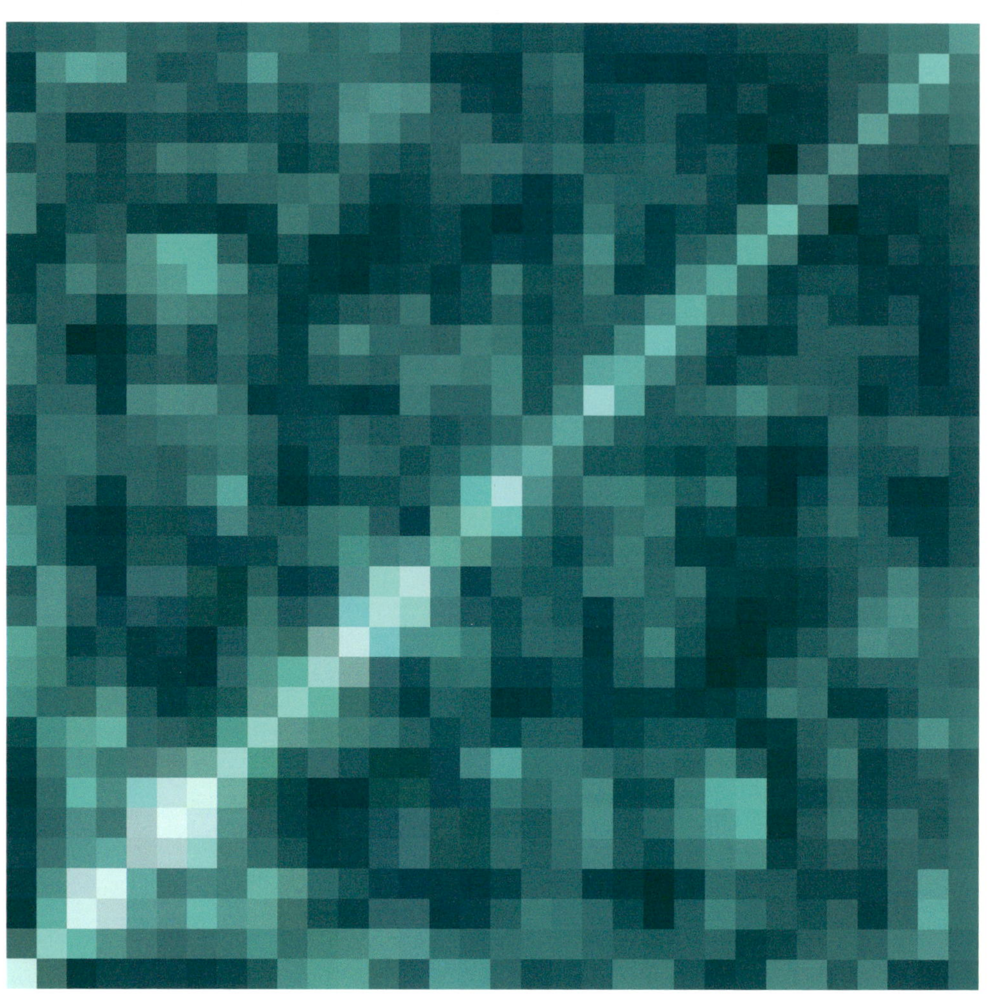

Resynthesizers	0.1
Matrice	18660
Scale	4:1

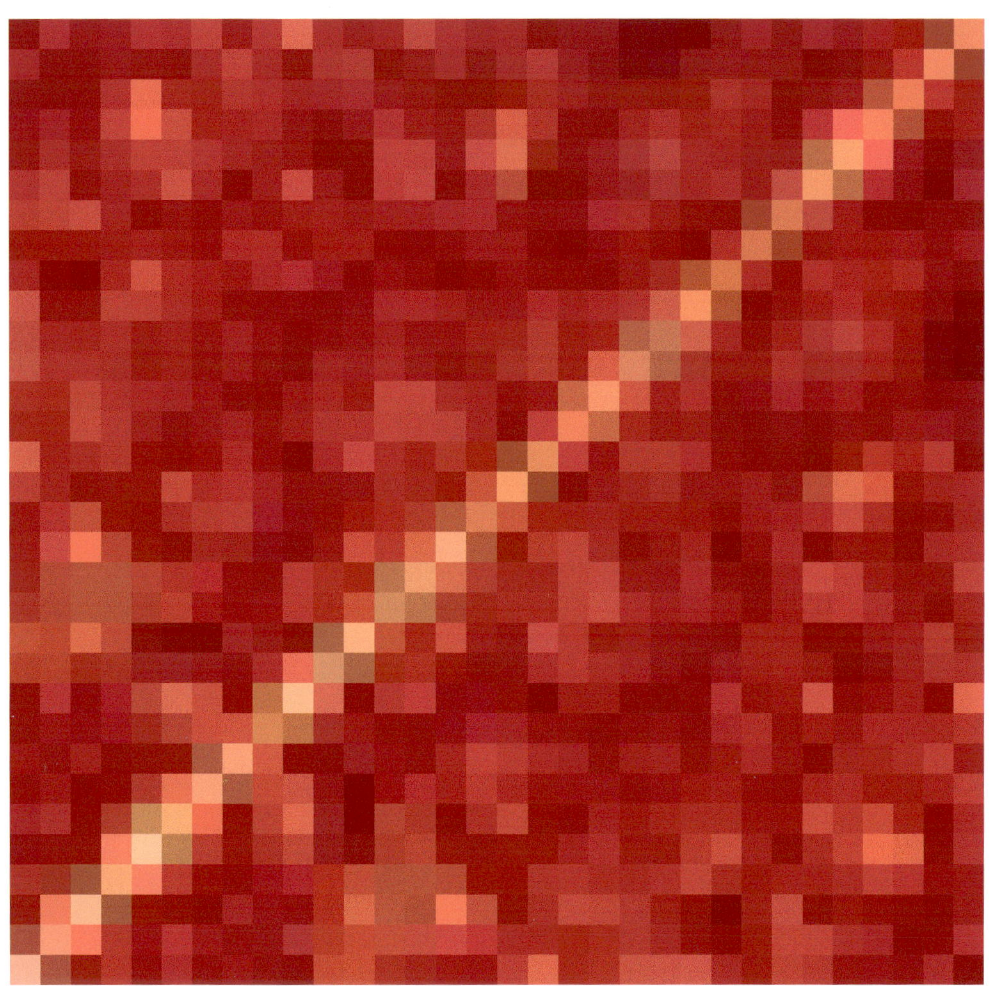

Resynthesizers	0.2
Matrice	15861
Scale	4:1

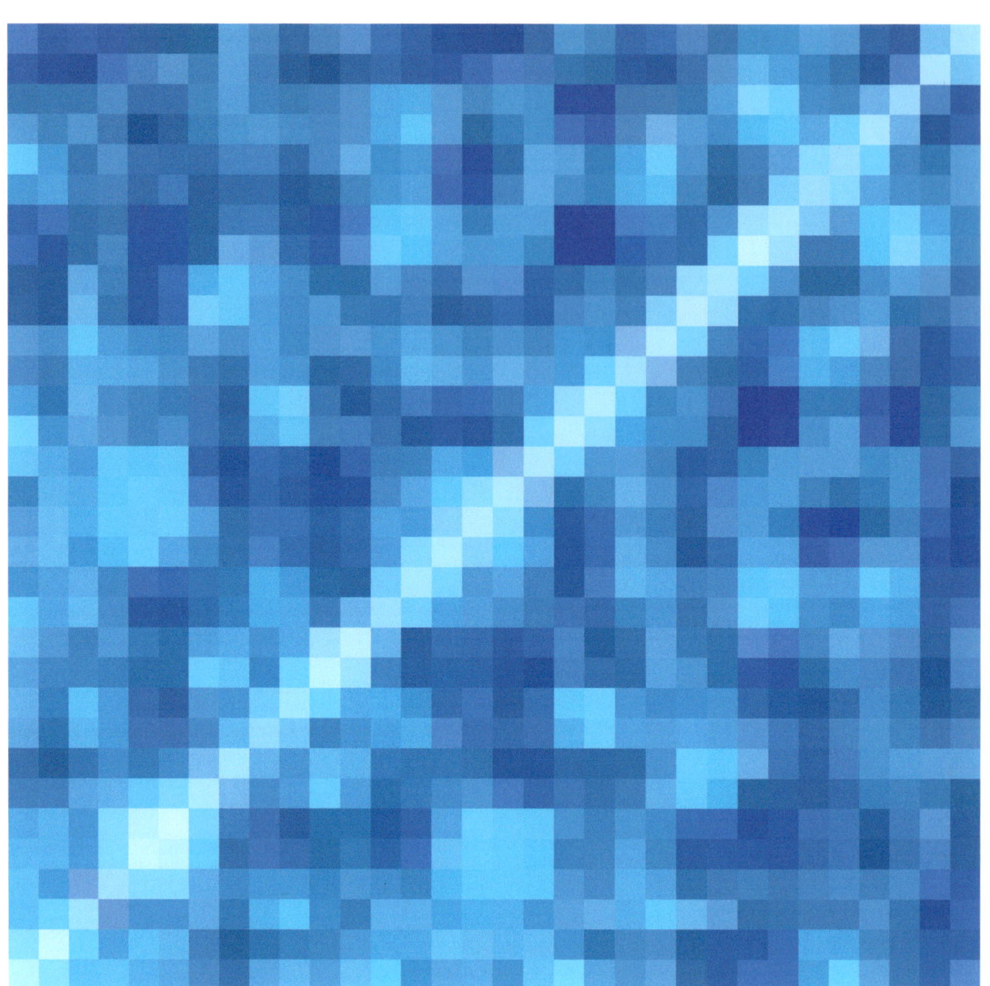

Resynthesizers	0.3
Matrice	12129
Scale	4:1

Resynthesizers	0.1
Matrice	18660
Scale	8:1

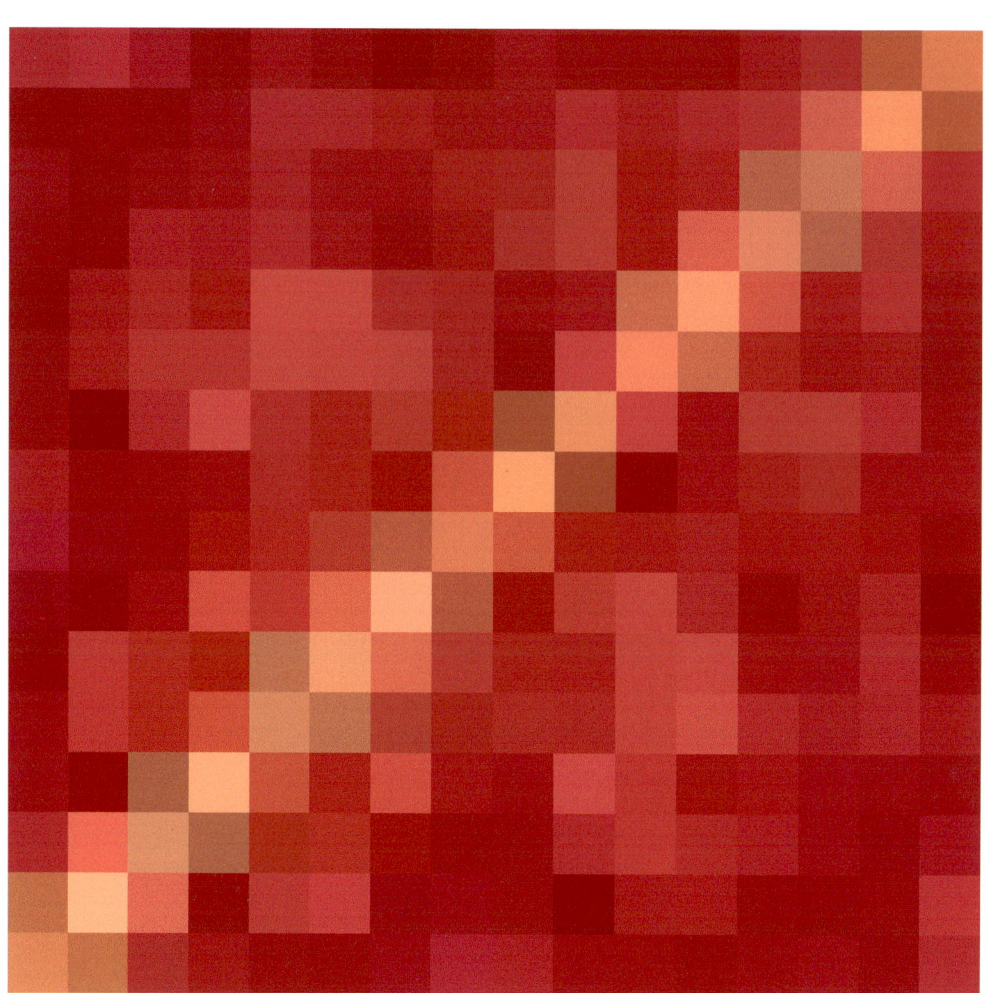

Resynthesizers	0.2
Matrice	15861
Scale	8:1

Resynthesizers	0.3
Matrice	12129
Scale	8:1

Resynthesizers	0.1
Matrice	18660
Scale	16:1

Resynthesizers	0.2
Matrice	15861
Scale	16:1

Resynthesizers	0.3
Matrice	12129
Scale	16:1

Resynthesizers	0.1
Matrice	18660
Scale	32:1

Resynthesizers	0.2
Matrice	15861
Scale	32:1

Resynthesizers	0.3
Matrice	12129
Scale	32:1

Resynthesizers	0.1
Matrice	18660
Scale	64:1

Resynthesizers	0.2
Matrice	15861
Scale	64:1

Resynthesizers	0.3
Matrice	12129
Scale	64:1

Resynthesizers	0.1
Matrice	18660
Scale	128:1

Resynthesizers	0.2
Matrice	15861
Scale	128:1

Resynthesizers 0.3
Matrice 12129
Scale 128:1

INSTALLATION VIEWS
FREDRIK NILSEN STUDIO

SCREENED LISTENING
MY GLOSS BODIES FORTH
TRIALS OF WRITING
MACHINE TONGUE 1985
DESTABILISING MARKERS

LINA
LINA
LINA
900-LFC

LINA
LINA
LINA
900-LFC

AROMATIC NUCLEUS
ICE CREAM ON THE BEACH
VAST METALLIC TIDE
INCOMPLETE COMPOUND
AND THE NAME

LINA

EXTENDED SPECTRAL TERRAIN
COMPONENT ARTIFICE
CONTINUOUS TEMPLEXTURE
EVENTLESS DYNAMISM
SCANNED FOR SALIENCIES

LINA
LINA
900-LFC

CORPOREAL COMMS MEMORIES
UNLISTED OF CHANEL
MAMAS AND ANOTHER
NOW ADRIFT TRANSITING
CYBERNETIC RESORT

IMPOSSIBLE SYNOPSIS
THIS READABLE MESSAGE
OUR ENDLESS SCROLL
THESE BROKEN IMPRESSIONS
SUBSTRING COMPONENT

LINA
LINA
LINA
900-LFC

Exhibition

Florian Hecker – Resynthesizers
November 21, 2021 – March 13, 2022
Fitzpatrick–Leland House
MAK Center for Art and Architecture
Los Angeles, CA
Organized by Equitable Vitrines

List of works
Resynthesizers 0.1
Resynthesizers 0.2
Resynthesizers 0.3
All: duration variable, 2021, 12-channel computer generated sound, software, Meyer Sound LINA line array loudspeaker system

Sound synthesis algorithm
Axel Röbel and members of the Analysis/Synthesis team, IRCAM, Paris

Sound computation
Cirrus UK National Tier-2 HPC Service at EPCC (www.cirrus.ac.uk) funded by the University of Edinburgh and EPSRC (EP/P020267/1)

Sound spatialisation design
Alberto de Campo

Libretti
Robin Mackay

Scent
Marc vom Ende & Philip Kraft, Symrise

Acknowledgments
Hecker wishes to thank Equitable Vitrines for their commitment to the project. Special thanks to Alberto de Campo, Marc vom Ende, Philip Kraft, Robin Mackay and Axel Röbel for their collaboration and contributions and to Wendy Hui Kyong Chun, Alex H. Barnett and Luciana Parisi. Sincere appreciation to James Perry and EPCC, The University of Edinburgh and Urbanomic, and NORM for their input on the typographic formatting of the e-ink displays.

Urbanomic urbanomic.com
Equitable Vitrines equitablevitrines.com

Equitable Vitrines

Publication

Editor
Equitable Vitrines

Copy Editing
Maya B. Kronic

Design
NORM, Zurich

Printer
DZA Druckerei zu Altenburg GmbH, Germany

Paper
MaxiSatin 135gsm

Typeface
LL Riforma (lineto.com)

All photographic images: 'Florian Hecker—Resynthesizers,' Fitzpatrick–Leland House

MAK Center for Art and Architecture Los Angeles, CA, November 21, 2021 – March 13, 2022, courtesy of the artist

Photography
Fredrik Nilsen Studio, Los Angeles
pp. 25–37, 150–183 and backcover

Covariance matrices of CNN feature activations
Axel Röbel
pp. 61–147

Visualisations
Philip Kraft
pp. 12–15

Echoing Resynthesis
Alex H. Barnett
pp. 46–47

Published by
Urbanomic Meda Ltd., The Old Lemonade Factory, Windsor Quarry, Falmouth, TR11 3EX, United Kingdom

Distributed by
the MIT Press

ISBN 978-1-915103-14-7

This publication is made possible by the support of the Michael Asher Foundation, the United Plankton Charitable Trust, the Robin Hwajin Yoon Kim Foundation, Marc vom Ende and Philip Kraft, and the California Arts Council.

Resynthesizers was funded by the Mike Kelley Foundation for the Arts, the Graham Foundation for Advanced Studies in the Fine Arts, the Michael Asher Foundation, the University of Edinburgh, the Goethe-Institut Los Angeles, the Institut für Auslandsbeziehungen, the City of Los Angeles Department of Cultural Affairs, the Los Angeles County Department of Arts and Culture, the MAK Center for Art and Architecture, the Wilhelm Family Foundation, and the Kebok Foundation. Additional support was provided by Symrise AG, Digital View, Inc., and the Roy and Edna Disney/CalArts Theater (REDCAT).